COLLECTING PAPER MONEY

Collecting Paper Money

COLIN NARBETH

LONDON

© Colin Narbeth 1986
First published 1986

Typeset by Servis Filmsetting Ltd, Manchester
and printed and bound in Great Britain
by The Bath Press Ltd
Bath, Somerset
for the publishers
B.A. Seaby Ltd
8 Cavendish Square
London W1M OAJ

Distributed by
B.T. Batsford Ltd
P.O. Box 4, Braintree
Essex CM7 7QY

ISBN 0-900-652-896

Contents

Acknowledgments

The author wishes to thank Raymond Sancroft-Baker and Elizabeth Norfolk of Christie's who provided many of the photographs of rare banknotes, and Robert J. Seaman, archivist of the Standard Chartered Bank, who also provided pictures and information. Thanks are also due to the Bank of England, the Bank of Scotland and the Bank of Ireland, who sanctioned publication.

I

Forming a Collection of Paper Money

Collectors are people with inquisitive, active minds. The great centres of learning and study, the world's museums, would be half empty if it were not for collectors of the past who have donated or sold their collections to them. Today they can be studied by new generations. And new generations, encouraged by collectors of the past, develop their own collections and add to the general fund of knowledge.

Collectors are sometimes criticised as hoarders and misers; and no doubt some are; but the vast majority are people with an interest in the world about them. Some just want to collect and appreciate fine art without necessarily having to involve themselves in a lot of study. They perform a useful function in preserving the material safely for future generations who may find it rewarding to study. Some collect as an investment. There is no reason why they should not, but it would be far safer to put the money in a building society. The main investment value a collector gets is the years of pleasure the hobby gives him; and the distinct probability of a longer, happier life. Those people who leave work at sixty-five and the next day don't know what to do with themselves have a bleak future. Those who keep their minds active with a hobby, or for that matter a sport, are more likely to live a long, happy life. That has got to be the best investment a person can make!

You will read in the media of great collectors whose collections have sold for massive figures. Not so news-worthy are the thousands of collections that fetch below the price that the collector paid. The odds are that a careful, discerning collector will be well rewarded when the collection is sold. But fashions change, hoards are discovered, and items are suddenly found to be forgeries – all affecting the value of a collection.

Least likely to succeed are the pure investors. They want to buy something and take it off the market so that you, the true collector, will have to pay more for it later on. They go to dealers and openly ask what there is in stock that is likely to 'double in value next year'. Dealers find them hard to resist! They don't know anything about the subject and they want to make money on someone else's skills. It never seems to occur to them that if a dealer knew something was going to double in value in a year's time, the very last thing that dealer would do is sell it for half of its potential value. They might let a collector have it at a discount. The collector is going to be a customer for a long time and the better deal he gets, the more likely he is to go back to that dealer.

So the best advice is to approach forming a collection without financial motivation. Form a collection because it is interesting and enjoyable. Naturally the collector must take account of value. It is no good paying £500 for a note just because you like it, if in fact you can buy it everywhere else for £100. The collector likes to know that he is paying somewhere in the region of the true market value. This only comes with experience and it must be said that when dealing with the great rarities of the world the value is simply what someone is prepared to pay. Dealers do not in fact decide what the value of an item is; the collector makes the final decision.

Newcomers to banknote collecting often experience the feeling of being in a maze. Most did not realise how fascinating the hobby is and tend to want to collect everything in sight. Indeed the hardest thing for any collector to do is to stick to a chosen path and not get side-tracked into starting other collections. Only the very strongest minds fail to develop some 'side-lines'.

The best way to mitigate this is to start off making a general collection of the world, with two qualifications. Only obtain inexpensive notes and only get them in extremely fine condition or better. The purpose of such a collection is to give you 'a feel' for what exists in the hobby, and in a very short time your own preferences will begin to assert themselves. Starting off from scratch blindly picking a subject can be disastrous, as later on the collector might find another area, which he did not know existed, is far more interesting to him. If he has spent a great deal of money on his first choice, he might have problems trying to sell them after such a short time. But by choosing inexpensive notes in excellent condition he will have learned the range of the hobby for a little outlay and, as the notes are in top condition, they will not be difficult to re-sell.

It is not a practical proposition to try and collect a meaningful collection of the notes of the world. Only the Gettys of this world can even consider such an idea. But that is not to say that one cannot have a representative collection of the world's issues. If such a collection is based on a period of, say, ten years, like 1939 to 1949, the collection, while big, would be able to be representative. For those who like general collecting, there are possibilities with the art side of notes. A collection of beautifully engraved notes of the world can be as large or small as the collector wishes and still demonstrate the artistic skills of the engravers. Collecting examples by different printing houses of the world can lead to a massive collection.

The advantage of that type of collecting is that wherever one goes, in antique shops, numismatic markets, etc., there is likely to be something of interest. The difficulty with that type of collecting is that it is never likely to be more than representative. Most collectors like to achieve a form of completeness – a comprehensive collection.

This can be done, for example, by choosing a country to collect, or a group of countries. The choice of country is better made if one has formed a general world collection first. For now the collector will know which countries have a lot of notes, which have only a few, and whether they are basically very expensive or inexpensive. The choice must be dictated to some extent by the purse of the collector. It is no good trying to form a collection of Sarawak, where most notes cost over £1,000, if your income cannot meet such expenditure. People with a small budget could well choose Germany, China, Russia or Brazil. In such countries inflation has left large quantities of very attractive notes at low prices, while at the same time there is a range of medim-priced scarce notes and great rarities. Young collectors in particular should never be put off by the fact that the country of their choice has great rarities. By the time they have collected all the common notes together they might well be in a position to get the scarcer ones; and if they have built up some duplicates they might do this by part exchange.

Some collectors, however well-off they may be, simply don't want to be expected to lay out a lot of money for their collection; they want a fun collection that is not going to make financial demands on them. There is plenty to collect in the paper money world, such as *notgeld* (emergency city notes produced in Germany) and inflation notes, in the cases of Germany, Greece, Hungary, Russia and others.

Since the exchange controls were lifted a few years ago a new form of collecting paper money has developed; modern currencies of the world, the low values of which are comparatively inexpensive. The major advantage to the new collector is that he is getting a 'face' value, cashable at a bank; and has only really laid out the percentage over face which he has had to pay to get the note. If he has collected them on holiday abroad, he has not even got that to pay. With some countries he will see his value disappearing fast – in 1985 Israel, Bolivia and Argentina saw banknote issues drop in face value at an alarming rate. But with other countries the collector may well score. When a leader is deposed, which seems to happen frequently, the new regime often bans and destroys the notes bearing the portrait of the deposed president. They can become scarce overnight.

There are many collectors who find enjoyment in the 'jigsaw' kind of collecting. That is to say, they want to complete in detail a section of notes. Notes are issued with prefix letters, not necessarily in alphabetical order, and often with signature changes made during the use of the same prefix letter. It is a popular form of collecting and allows an achievement of 'completeness' when one can get a whole series together.

Such collecting is fairly expensive as many of the British notes are rare and worth a great deal more than face value. But the same pleasure of 'jig-saw' collecting can be obtained in less expensive fields for those limited by finance. Collecting German inflation notes by different prefixes and numbering systems can give the same enjoyment for much less cost. There is a lot of merit in choosing a less popular area because the cost will be lower and the likelihood is that the area might become popular later on. German East African one rupie notes are a good example. Often these can be bought for from 50p to £1.50 each. There is a maze of different serial prefixes, not to mention type-face sizes and signatures. The early notes are handsigned by officials and the whole lot were produced under wartime emergency conditions using all sorts of paper from letter-heads to ammunition wrapping paper. Specialist collectors can often find very scarce items priced as normal issues.

Subject collecting is also very popular. One of the reasons theme collecting is so popular is that it can be as simple as merely collecting banknotes with pictures of animals on them, or as detailed as tracing the development of medicine through banknotes; indeed major international awards have been won by a collector of medicine on paper money. Apart from those which simply bear pictures related to medicine, there are notes issued by hospitals, issued for leper colonies, and so on.

The individual collector has to decide for himself what he wants out of the hobby. Perhaps he does not want to devote too much time to the hobby and is content to get together a small but valuable collection of rarities. Others may want to devote a lot of their free time to the hobby without becoming bankrupt in the process. Such collectors need to pick an area where the material is abundant. In the philatelic world there is a saying that it is no good setting out to 'plate' Penny Blacks unless you are fairly well off, but you can get exactly the same pleasure by plating penny reds for a fraction of the cost. The same applies to banknotes.

Specialisation is the best way of forming a meaningful collection and, by dogged research and study, being in a position to pick up rarities inexpensively. The disadvantage is that as the collection grows, the ability to add to it gets less and less. A happy solution for most collectors is to have a range. They pick a country or a subject for a general collection. Then they choose an area of that subject for specialised treatment; and at the same time they choose a theme as a side-line. It ensures that wherever they go there is likely to be something of interest for them. But it does have the disadvantage of spreading the available finances!

There are plenty of areas which are almost 'virgin' territories for research in the paper money world. For example, cheques, postal orders (although several works have been published on English postal orders, just about nothing is known about foreign postal orders), and financial ephemera, for example, traveller's cheques. Most of these are areas where a great deal of material is available for the patient researcher. There are also areas, like the very early paper money of the UK, the goldsmith notes, which need a lot of attention. There are pioneer collectors in this field, but the majority of collectors cannot easily distinguish a true goldsmith note from an ordinary promissory note. Such items tend to be expensive, but most of the existing specialist collectors find they pick some up for next to nothing because the vendor thought they were ordinary cheques. The pleasure of researching the history of the note-issuers is often very rewarding and unearths little known historical facts.

Fortunately for the collecting world, everyone has different ideas – if we all wanted to collect the same thing there would not be much of it around to find. So you hear 'I don't understand prefix collecting, they must be mad', 'I only want issued notes, I don't think specimens are real notes', 'I like my notes to be slightly circulated, to have been used for the purpose they were made', 'I only want them perfect'. No-one is right or wrong. Collect what you like, what gives you the most pleasure. If you make it an interesting, informative collection, the chances are that other people looking at it will want to collect them as well.

2

Condition and Cleaning

Condition

The condition of a note is more a matter of opinion than an exact science. There are certain guide-lines laid down by past collectors who have found them satisfactory, but, as is often the case, there are more than one set of guide-lines. One system works on points. It starts out with 100 for perfect and deducts 5 points for a crease, 10 for a tear, and so on. The problem is that the position of a dirt smudge can make a lot of difference. If it is on the face of the portrait shown on the note, it affects the value much more than if it is in a corner margin.

The most popular system is that which the British Museum adopts for numismatics. This starts with Poor, which simply means that the item is severely damaged. As a general rule it also indicates that a collector will not want such a note because its condition tends to spoil the effect of a page of better notes. The next grade is Good, and this in fact is a misnomer. It actually means 'bad'. Such notes are badly damaged but they qualify as 'good' because the printed design is complete, i.e. there may be bits missing from the edges of the note, but not from the actual design. Then comes Very Good, again a misnomer, because it means not quite so bad as good! It will have small tears and stains, pinholes, etc.

While those first three conditions should be avoided by the new collector, it is a different matter for experienced specialists. A collector of Sarawak who comes across a fragment of a note which pre-dates all known issues and has never been seen before, is going to treat it with reverence and mount it very carefully to illustrate the point that there was an earlier issue than hitherto recorded. From his point of view the condition of the note is nowhere near so important as the historical fact that it demonstrates. He will know that he is unlikely to get another.

But the new collector cannot be expected to know which notes are available in better grades. There are notes which because of inflation or change of government are available in very large quantities in perfect condition for 50p each or even less. To have a poor note of that type is quite pointless. Until the new collector can get the feel of his hobby and build up a knowledge of what is and what is not available in certain conditions, he is well advised to leave the lower grades alone. Many collectors start out with the accent on quantity rather than quality, and buy lots of bad condition notes because they are cheap, only to find later on that nobody else wants them.

A good rule of thumb is to refuse any note below the condition of Fine, which is the next grade. Grades of Fine and above have one thing in common; they are appealing. There is no severe damage to mar the look of the note. A note which qualifies as Fine will show substantial evidence of circulation – folds, creases and perhaps small stains – but the combined effect of these faults does not detract from the overall attractive appearance of the note.

Most collectors who have some experience in the hobby will accept a scarce note in Fine condition because the price differential will be sufficient to warrant it. For example, a note in Fine condition might be £30, whereas in perfect condition it could be £300. Many have no choice because they cannot afford to spend £300 on any note, but they might be able to scrape up the £30 and have a reasonable example of it.

Apart from currently circulating notes and those notes which exist in large quantities, the condition Very Fine is satisfactory to the majority of collectors. This means a note which though it shows obvious signs of circulation, multiple folds etc., is otherwise undamaged and appealing.

Then comes Extremely Fine and the difference between this and Very Fine is that there are only the slightest signs of circulation; perhaps a centre fold, or a crease mark left by a banker's thumb as he counted a pile of notes. It should have an uncirculated quality about it, have that crispness of a new note and look very desirable to a collector. Many catalogues give this as the highest grade for very early issues of paper money.

The terms discussed so far are abbreviated in numismatic works as P (Poor); G (Good); VG (Very Good); F (Fine); VF (Very Fine) and EF (Extremely Fine). American catalogues often use the term XF for EF.

The top grade in paper money is Uncirculated. This means

absolutely perfect. If you can find a blemish on the note then it is not Uncirculated, it is Extremely Fine. The term needs a bit of explanation. The numismatic grading system has FDC (Fleur de Coin) as its top condition. But because modern methods of minting coins result in 'bag scratches' , it is not possible to describe the majority of modern coins as FDC, even though they may not have circulated at all. So the term Uncirculated was introduced to show the difference between a truly beautiful FDC and a modern minted coin. To the coin collector, the term Uncirculated means that it does have defects. The paper money collector can hardly use the term FDC, which relates specifically to coin, to indicate the top grade, so the term Uncirculated was adopted to mean FDC in the paper money world.

Major catalogues of paper money give detailed definitions of the conditions they use and their interpretation of them. The collector is advised always to study such catalogue definitions carefully. It will become apparent that personal judgements are not necessarily the same. Singularly obvious to the new collector will be the considerable number of dealers who contend a note is VF when they are buying it, and EF when they are selling it!

The confusion comes with adjectival additions. Notes will be (perhaps correctly) described as 'nearly VF', 'about VF', 'VF +', 'Good Fine'. Most dealers do this, but tend to give themselves the benefit of any doubt! If the new collector sticks to the basic terms he will not go far wrong. If he doubts that a note is EF then he should take the view that it is VF for the practical purpose of buying it. If he feels that it really is a 'VF +' (plus), then he will not mind the dealer asking a little more for it. It is a bargaining point.

One thing the new collector should beware is the practice (more common in the coin world) of a dealer maintaining that an item is EF 'for this particular item', suggesting that as it is of a particular age, or great rarity, it is comparable to an EF condition of a more modern item. This is pure nonsense. Condition has nothing to do with rarity or age.

An appreciation of condition is vital because it affects the value of the item. Catalogues like Pick (Standard Catalogue of World Paper Money) use three conditions for each note to give readers an idea of value: G (Good) or VG (Very Good) to represent the lower grades, F (Fine) or VF (Very Fine) to indicate the average condition and EF (Extremely Fine) or UNC (Uncirculated) for top grade. The lower grades are used for very early issues of notes and the higher grades for more modern issues.

Taking an actual example from the fifth edition of Pick: United States 1 dollar, Pick 351, is $65 in VG, $125 in VF and $400 in UNC. The value of the note shows such considerable differences for condition that it is essential to judge it accurately.

The same series of notes of the United States also demonstrates that VG (Very Good) is well worth collecting for some notes, e.g. Pick 357 (a $100 note of 1891), which is $6,000 in VG, $13,000 in VF and unpriced in UNC. The majority of notes in VG, however, are lowly priced and tend to fetch less than catalogue value, whereas a considerable number of notes fetch higher than catalogue in EF and UNC.

Never be afraid to ask a dealer for the condition of a note which he is offering you. Just say you are new to the hobby and trying to learn. Most will be helpful and tell you why they have judged it to be a certain condition. The one or two who will say 'It's as it is – you can see it, decide for yourself' are really telling you that they don't know, or know very well they have priced it for a higher grade than it is. If they claim to be professional dealers, then they should know. Of course, an antique dealer with a box of notes cannot be expected to know, but at least the new collector is aware that he is in a high risk area. Experienced collectors like such an area because they can pick up bargains – but the new collector will likely find that he could have bought the same note for half the price from a specialist banknote dealer. There are more 'bad buys' than 'bargains' on offer from the non-professional banknote dealers.

There are collectors who will accept nothing unless it is perfect. I disagree with this viewpoint but accept that my view is a personal one and open to dispute. An Extremely Fine note should look almost new and have no unsightly blemishes. Such a note is pleasing to look at. To now argue that it is not quite perfect – and therefore not good enough – is a mentality which defeats the object of forming a collection of anything other than condition. Notes do not exist in such perfect condition in quantities that allow a meaningful collection to be formed.

The object of forming a collection is to achieve an end product which tells a story, educates and informs. There is a danger that condition-mania can override the purpose of a true collection. Experience teaches us that many notes are very hard to find in any condition. The older we get, the more often we hear the familiar moan of experience: 'I saw that once, but I didn't take it because it was in bad condition – wish I had now'. So, my plea to a new collector is to guard against condition-mania. Don't refuse a lovely, fascinating historical item just because a corner has a crease in it. In my view there is only one major question the collector need ask himself: 'Is it pleasing?' Rejecting an item simply because it is not perfect is to destroy your chances of forming a good collection. Only a very limited collection can be made of flawless items – of any subject.

Cleaning

Most of the world's famous museums have departments whose sole function is to restore, clean and preserve items. Specialist experts are employed to preserve old documents and fragments of ancient manuscripts. The object is not to make the item look better in order to attract a higher value, but to ensure that it can still be examined and studied a hundred years from now.

The collector is going to be offered material that has been cleaned, and he should be very wary. The majority of those 'doctoring' the notes are not experienced museum specialists, but people trying to make the note fetch more money by turning a VF item into EF. More often than not, they do more harm to the note. There are tell-tale signs which, while not necessarily an indication of cleaning, justify a more thorough examination.

First, sometimes the note will appear limp; the result of washing. But of course some countries did officially wash and re-circulate their notes at certain times, for example Portugal and the United States. Sometimes the note will curl; the result of ironing. Look for a 'glisten' on the note caused by an iron, and examine under a glass the fibre of the edges – nine times out of ten the person with the iron will have pressed the fibres down in different directions. Experts will get round this by taking a long time to dry the paper after washing, literally several weeks of slow drying, and will iron with heavy material between the note and the iron.

Many people would argue that there is not a lot wrong with

such processes. If a note has a dried jam stain on it, the best thing to do would be to take it off. Dealers on the continent and in the Far East often pencil the price on in the top margins; most people would use an ordinary rubber and erase the price. But most collectors would like to know if the note they are buying has been treated in any way. It probably would not stop them buying the note – but it might affect the price.

There are more dangerous methods of cleaning, which, fortunately, the new collector can usually identify. Smell the note. Chemical treatment (unless professionally done in a way that does not harm paper) will leave a distinct smell, as against mustiness, caused by long-term storage. The best advice is don't buy the note. The chemical reaction on the paper may well disintegrate it in a few years' time.

One has to be a little careful over this point because some dealers keep the notes in inferior pockets which have acids in them. They transfer to the paper, and give the chemical smell. Usually that smell will totally disappear in a few minutes once the note is taken out and air allowed to circulate round it. But the only reason the note is not damaged is that it has not been in the holder long enough to absorb sufficient of the chemicals. If a note has been in such a container for several years it might be a different story. Now that manufacturers are producing special containers for paper money which are acid free, the majority of dealers will eventually use them – though of course they are two or three times more expensive at the moment.

If the note has passed the test of smelling, holding on the palm of the hand to see if it curls and not being unusually limp, it does not follow that it has not been 'doctored' by an efficient person. Hold the note up to a strong light and look through the reverse side of the note. If at any time that note has been creased and the crease pressed out, there will usually be a tell-tale faint line. Now pass the note through finger and thumb exerting enough pressure to see if your touch senses a ridge. If the note passes both tests the chances are that it is perfectly okay, and even if it is not the probability is that it doesn't much matter! It will have been done by a trained professional whose job is to restore without damaging in any way.

Don't miss the obvious. If the colour seems wrong, check it against a similar note. On occasion the note will appear duller or faded for the simple reason that it has been stuck in a shop window and taken the full glare of the sun for a few weeks. The average collector would pass such a note. A good indication of a note in excellent condition is the crispness of the paper, 'the crackle of new notes'. One does not expect to find this with old notes, but for modern issues it is a good guide.

It would be wrong not to point out that notes in VF condition can be made into EF by experts at paper preservation and restoration. It takes a long time, as they have to analyse the inks, the structure of the paper, etc. But notes firmly stuck down on card can be taken off, the creases taken out, and the note restored to EF condition. No harm has been done to the note. Only a scientist would ever be able to find out that the note had been treated at all. It happens all the time to rare and valuable manuscripts in the world's museums. It costs a lot of money and such processes would not be worth using unless the note was valuable.

The note can be re-sized to restore the crackle, oxidisation removed, the lot. The point of mentioning all this is to offset to some degree the condition-mania. Paying £5,000 for a 'perfect' note as against £1,500 for the same note VF could be paying £1,000 for restoration work and giving the vendor another £2,500!

In the end collecting condition is a matter of personal choice. Most people would like to have an item as perfect as possible and the restriction on them is usually financial. There is nothing wrong with seeking perfection. It has been said by several dealers, 'Well, if you can't tell it has been cleaned, what does it matter?' But the professionals can tell, and it does matter as far as the price is concerned.

19

3

Dealers, Auction Houses and Other Hunting Grounds

Collecting paper money is not just a matter of paying out money and getting lots of notes. For one thing, the rarities of the world are not there just for the taking. The experienced collector soon finds that even some notes which are common, according to catalogue prices, are not at all easy to find. Locating the item is sometimes more difficult than finding the money to pay for it. Indeed some of the major dealing houses have orders to 'buy' certain items for wealthy customers. The price is not important to the customer; obtaining the item is. But the dealing house has to find it.

Dealers

It is often said that the major dealing houses are more expensive. It is not in fact true. Very often the opposite is the case; they employ top experts who often value less than perfect condition at very much less than other dealers. They get the reputation for high prices simply because they tend to sell the world's top rarities which, of course, fetch top prices. The new collector should not be put off by the magnificence of the buildings or top-hatted doormen. Such firms are interested in collectors and they will help them. Naturally they cannot afford to have customers regularly looking through the whole stock and ending up buying something for 50p, after half a day. But once they know you are a serious collector and that you will buy if they have the right item at a fair price, then you will be treated as a regular customer and items put aside for you to look at. One of the great advantages of going to the major dealers is that you can always go back. If the item turns out to be wrong they will be the first to take it back and refund it, but the chances of it being a dud are very much less than when buying in the general market.

The best source for the specialist collector is the professional dealer who specialises in paper money. The new collector should make a point of going through the stocks of all the dealers he can manage to visit. He will learn what is available to purchase and at what price. In no time he will find that some dealers charge more than others; some dealers grade differently from others, and so on. Generally, he will find that dealers tend to have certain items priced higher than average and other items priced below average. The reason for this is that most dealers price up according to cost. If they bought low then they will pass some of the benefit on to their customers. This is not because they are particularly philanthropic; it is just good business sense. The customer who gets a 'good deal' comes back again. It is often said that a dealer never really minds making a mistake and selling an item worth £50 for £5 because the lucky collector is going to tell all his friends – who are going to rush round to see what they can find! It is a good advertisement.

Where the true collector comes into his own with the paper money dealer is when he collects a specific and somewhat complicated area, like German notgeld, Philippine guerilla notes, Indonesia revolutionary notes or inflation notes. Most of these tend to be fairly inexpensive but, of course, there are many varieties and a few rarities. The dealer cannot afford to sort through a couple of thousand notgeld to find half a dozen that are worth £5 each instead of 25p. By the time he has sorted and studied them, he has put that amount of money into the effort. So the collector, whose time is free, can happily sort through for hours and pick them out. But he does have to have the technical knowledge which takes time to build up. The dealer has to have a general knowledge of the world and cannot possibly know as much as a specialist.

One of the better ways of meeting dealers is to go to the International Bank Note Society meetings, or the major coin shows which paper money dealers attend. The advantage is that a number of dealers are in the same place. The collector can find a note in a dealer's stock, and then go round the other dealers to see if any of them have a better condition note or a cheaper one in the same condition. Also, he will see a greater variety of notes than he would at an individual dealer's shop.

There are not that many dealers in the United Kingdom and the collector will soon get to know them all. They all advertise in the coin magazines and most are members of the important organisations (see Appendix A). Specialist collectors will want to seek out dealers who also specialise in their particular areas. Whereas you might pick up a variety from a dealer who does not realise he has it and therefore get it inexpensively, it is also true that scarce varieties are not at all easy to find. A specialist dealer is more likely to have one. So we find established dealers like Eddie Prigg who has a better-than-most knowledge of Japanese hansatsu notes; David Keable and Enid Salter, generally acknowledged as the top experts on British notes; Yasha Beresiner, specialist in the Ottaman Empire, and so on. The collector will soon find which dealers specialise in particular areas. Of course they all sell notes of the world, but they often have specific areas in which they excel. Some have been in the 'business' a long time and are also collectors themselves, dealers like Brian Kemp, who has a superb collection of goldsmith notes and specialises in Victorian period issues of the old British Empire; Michael O'Grady, Irish specialist, and David Gyles who has studied early American issues for many years. It is not possible to mention them all, but the collector who joins the IBNS and gets their literature and reads the coin magazines will soon find out which dealers are well known for particular subjects.

All the professional dealers are going to give the customer what they think is a 'fair deal'. It is not a question of any great morality; just common sense. Rather than make an 'extra few bucks' off a new collector, they would prefer you to be satisfied and come back again, and hopefully again and again. That way they will make a good living. The customer who is 'caught', soon gets to know and simply does not go back to that particular dealer.

There are customers who make a point of only dealing with one dealer, and these include some of the world's really big collectors. Even if they see a note they want in someone else's stock, they don't buy it. They go to their dealer and tell him to get it – that dealer will naturally get a trade discount, so everyone is happy. The reasoning behind it all is that the customer knows his dealer is going to give him the best possible deal, as he is a regular source of income and needs to be treated very well. However, most collectors get a lot of enjoyment from going round and finding the notes for themselves. The one-dealer customers tend to be those who are extremely busy people and just don't have the time to spare.

The new collector does not have to confine himself to dealers in paper money. He can find banknotes in all sorts of odd places: antique shops, second-hand shops, and market stalls. Coin fairs are good hunting grounds; very often coin dealers will have a small bundle of notes which they had to buy in order to get the coins they wanted. However, the collector needs to be wary. It is no reflection on the dealer, who may be a top expert in antiques or coins, but he is not an expert in paper money. Very often it is a 'one-off', so the dealer is not expecting you to be a regular customer. The tendency is therefore to get as much as he can.

The end result is that the specialist collector finds such places a very interesting hunting ground. The new collector can find bargains – or a costly trap. In a bunch of notes on an antique stall it is sometimes possible to find notes at £5 which are worth £20 among knowledgeable banknote dealers; it is also possible to find notes at £5 which any professional dealer will sell you for 50p. No-one can blame the seller. He is usually the first to say he doesn't know anything about them. In his own interests he tends to value them as high as he can. The experienced collectors will go through the stocks of these shops and then visit the banknote dealers; the new collector is better off going to the banknote dealer until he knows the true values.

Catalogue prices are a good guide, but are not always correct. What happens is that a hoard turns up of a note which was previously thought to be scarce. This happened recently with Ghana and Equatorial Guinea – in the latter case with a note cataloguing at $250 and now worth about £40. It never hurts to ask the dealer, if there is a doubt in your mind, if there is a hoard of the note you are buying. It will soon become apparent if there is a hoard out, so the dealer is on the spot if he says 'No'. The established dealer is usually the first to tell his customers when a hoard is on the market, but there are dealers who try and slip two or three at a time into the market at prices no longer justifiable. The collector will not take long to find out and such dealers tend to go out of business after a while.

Auction houses

Another very important source for the collector is the auction houses. Major London auction houses like Christie's, Sotheby's and Phillips' often have specialised sales of paper money or a number of lots in a coin auction. There is always an element of excitement about buying in an auction. The lucky buyer finds that no-one else is interested in a particular lot and he gets it for much less than he was prepared to pay. It also works the other way when two or three collectors are after a very rare item and are prepared to pay way over the estimate. Some of the unique Bradbury archive material at Christie's, estimated in hundreds, went for thousands. At the end of the day an item is worth what a collector will pay for it.

If you buy from a reputable auction house, at least you know there was an under-bidder. Someone else was prepared to pay almost as much. But it is dangerous to assume that auction realisations can be used as guides to value. At a recent auction a dealer had put in an item which had been sitting in his stock for a year marked at £500. In auction it went for over £2,000. Sometimes high prices are fetched because a particular person wants it badly. It is not unknown for a wealthy collector to pay an enormous price simply to stop a 'friend' from having it! Catalogue compilers do take notice of auction realisations – but not one-offs. When an item has been in auction three or four times and consistently fetches between £100 and £150, then it will be accepted as a fair valuation. But if the item is only sold once it does not mean that it will fetch the same price again. Serious collectors of all subjects soon learn that auction prices can be erratic. The new collector should keep and file all the auction records he can. They make a good reference and give a price guide once a note has been sold several times.

Collectors who do this find that the very same note often turns up a few years later in another auction house, or even the same auction house. The owner may have died or decided to sell it. The general trend is for such items to fetch more the second time; but not always. It is through this sort of study that a collector can build up a technical knowledge which helps him in his purchases.

Sometimes the note a collector wants is in a mixed lot and he is faced with the prospect of having to buy ten unwanted items to get the one he wants. At first the collector tends to think it is a nuisance, but there are advantages. Most dealers are going to leave the lot alone because they already have plenty of some of the notes in stock and would only have wanted one or two. A lot of collectors will leave them alone because they only want the one note. This means the lot may well go under the hammer at a low price. This is where the collector known in the trade as the 'dealer-collector' comes into his own. Having taken out the note he wanted, the dealer-collector now sets about trying to sell or exchange the others. Not infrequently he does very well and even ends up getting his note for nothing! It has been known for a collector to buy three or four lots this way and put the ones he did not want back into the next auction and come out of it with a good profit. It all depends on who attends the auction.

The dealer-collector can have quite a lot of fun, but he should remember that the professional dealer is more likely to have the better knowledge when it comes to that sort of business.

Other hunting grounds

There are other ways of acquiring notes than by purchase. Exchanging with fellow collectors can be rewarding. Most experienced collectors will help a new collector and may well, knowingly, give him a bargain. Specialist collectors may have a fair stock of duplicates and be delighted to exchange for something they want, giving twice the normal value in exchange because they obtained them cheaply by buying bulk in the first place. However, this is where the old warning of watching condition comes in. Some collectors will try hard to get rid of bad condition notes to a new collector. It is their only chance. By and large the new collector will find he is well treated by experienced collectors. In the long run it is always sensible to be fairly fluid in exchange dealing. There are collectors who will not part with a note from their collection at any price, but I think the sensible collector will. You cannot take it with you; you are only a custodian while you live, and the object is to form a collection – so if someone will pay a lot more than you expect for an item, it means you can use the money to buy other notes and enlarge your collection with equally interesting material.

There is another way of adding to a collection. When travelling abroad it always pays to look carefully at the foreign notes, and to keep a few in perfect condition. They can be good exchange material later on. There are collectors who only collect notes from places they have visited. For them a holiday is a hunting trip. There are collectors of British notes who regularly go round to banks in the High Street with their pay packet notes and change them to other denominations. That way the collector gets a chance to examine all sorts of prefix letters and numbers and it costs him nothing!

Exchanging by mail is also an interesting and useful method of collecting. It can also cause problems. Always register sendings so that lost mail is genuinely 'lost'. It never hurts to jot down the serial numbers of the notes you send – just in case some unscrupulous person tries to switch notes in order to get a better condition one for nothing. It does not often happen, but it has happened.

4
Writing-up a Collection

Those who have collected some notes with a discerning eye and have them in excellent condition now have the task of protecting them and 'writing them up' so that they can be displayed.

The most suitable method of storage is an album. There are many types of album available and it is largely a question of personal choice. But there are a number of points the collector should consider.

1 The pages, which are generally sold with one, two, three or four 'pockets' to contain the notes, need to be free from acids and harmful chemicals, if long-term protection is wanted. This means, unfortunately, that the pages tend to be expensive, on average 50p each. Some firms guarantee their pages to be free from acid, which more than anything else causes harm to paper, particularly where fugitive inks, as used in signatures, are concerned. It is most important that the collector does not use housing material which damages the notes. Notes kept in cheap albums with poor quality pages can develop a sort of white fungus on them after a year or two; the notes begin to smell of chemicals, and often the page material crinkles. It is far cheaper in the long run to pay more for quality.

The new collector can go along to a society meeting of paper money enthusiasts and see what other collectors use; or visit the archivist of a bank or musuem and see how their notes are housed. Often such institutions will have scientific tests made to ensure that the material they are using is safe.

2 According to what is being collected, the decision has to be made as to whether both sides of a note need to be shown. Normally they do; but of course specialists in early paper money where usually one side is blank may feel that only the obverse is worth showing. Also, collectors of modern notes may like to have two of each, so that an obverse and reverse of a note can be shown side by side. At first sight this is an expensive method of collecting;

but artistically it can be worthwhile for certain collections. Some people always collect in pair sequence. It is a national trait of Iranian collectors that all notes should be collected in sequence numbers where possible. If only one side of the note needs displaying, then there are a great many albums to choose from, and the best advice to a collector is to go to one of the major philatelic firms where they can see a wide range of such albums, which are used for collecting postcards, postal history and a number of subjects. They are ideal for paper money if only one side of a note needs display.

However, most collectors will want to show both sides of a note and this limits the choice to those types of album with clear 'pockets' to hold the notes. The one which seems the most popular in Europe is the Lindner banknote album, 30.5 by 31.7cm. It costs around £18.95, and can cost more with extra pages and slip case. However, pages to hold various numbers of notes go with it, which is important. A collector of notgeld would be content with four-slot pages and could house twelve to sixteen notes a page; whereas a collector of English white fivers would need two-slot pages. There are other very good quality albums like the Melinex, and this album is ideal for collectors of large size notes. But it does have only one size of page. Whereas the notes can be held in place by the suction of the page itself, there is a danger they will move about if the album is carelessly handled.

There are some very good albums on the market which cost under £10. They tend to be slightly smaller than the more expensive albums but will house ninety per cent of all issued notes. Stanley Gibbons Ltd, who are among the most experienced album producers in the world, have a very attractive new album which can be used by postal history or banknote collectors. There is also the 'Hendon' album, originally produced for collectors of cigarette cards, but perfectly satisfactory for banknotes and of good quality.

3 Consider the range of notes which fall into the area chosen to collect. Countries such as Russia, China and Spain have very large notes, often referred to among collectors as 'horse-blankets'. Some of the albums mentioned, like the Lindner, will hold most, but not all, of these large notes, so the collector who has a number of them needs a different type of album. These can be obtained from the Bond and Share collecting world, where some of the items are very large indeed in comparison with banknotes. The collector who wants very large albums – and they do permit a very attractive display – should get in touch with these specialist manufacturers. M. Veissid and Co. have been producing bond and share albums for years, and quite recently began producing pages suitable for cheques or banknotes which can be used in them.

All the albums mentioned are known to me to be free of any dangerous materials (as far as science can tell anyway); there are probably a lot more and the new collector would do well to go to a collectors' accessory shop and ask to see what range they have. It is worth taking time and trouble to find the right album for your purposes.

4 Certain types of collection don't really need albums at all. A specialist in German inflation notes who is collecting all the different serial letters and types of numbers is going to have, sometimes, perhaps a hundred of the same type of note, the only differences being in the serial letters. For such notes the most compact method of housing is a file-box containing the special acid-free pockets. Such pockets come in various sizes and are used by most of the professional banknote dealers who have large stocks to display to customers. They keep the note clean and safe and can be filed alphabetically with ease. They are not inexpensive, because of the high quality of the material, and cost around 20p each.

Writing-up the collection is one of the great pleasures of collecting. The ability of a collector, his skill at selection, and his general research can be judged by the finished product. Basically the collector is setting out to tell a story, illustrated by the notes themselves. It may be straightforward, like the note issues of a country in their order of appearance; or it may be the story of wartime emergency issues by military powers, with all the complicated background of the events at the time of issue.

As a general principle a write-up should be the same as a textbook. In other words, a complete newcomer to the subject should be able to read and understand what it is all about. The owner of the collection may know that a certain note is extremely rare, perhaps because the issue was confiscated, but a non-collector looking at it will not know; and the normal person would be interested in such details.

In writing-up, remember the standard rule for caption writers of pictures for newspapers and magazines. Say something the picture does not say. So if you are displaying a £1 note signed by the Chief Cashier, Beale, there is no need to write that, as it is on the note itself. But you can give the date of issue, the length of time for which the Chief Cashier signed the notes, how many were issued and a multitude of information which is not apparent from the note itself. That information is interesting, and adds to the attraction of the collection. Theme subjects, such as famous men portrayed on banknotes, give the collector an opportunity for as much, or as little, research as he likes. The public libraries provide all the reference works that are needed and the collector can turn his album into a book of knowledge. It goes without saying that the inquisitive collector gets as much pleasure in finding out about his notes as in having them. Perhaps more important, the collector can get as much pleasure from the hobby on a small budget as can the wealthy collector. Probably more, as the wealthy collector usually has not got the time to research his notes!

The hobby of banknote collecting is wide-open to the researcher. There were very few collectors until comparatively modern times and many note issues were 'lost' in history. Now students are beginning to find out about them and it makes the hobby quite fascinating. Numismatics is a subject which has been studied for a very long time and we have very precise knowledge of many coins issued hundreds of years BC. Yet in the banknote world we are still finding obscure note issues which were used within the last fifty years and have just been forgotten.

The write-up of a collection is worth all the time and effort, is part of the fun of the hobby, is a form of self-teaching, and is likely to add to the financial value of the collection.

It is always a good idea to make notes of where you obtained a note and how much you paid for it. At the time of purchase it may not seem very significant, but it can be important later. If the authenticity of an item is questioned, at least the collector will be able to trace where he obtained it, and it is both useful and interesting for the collector and his descendants to be able to check back on the cost of an item, in case the collection is to be sold.

Some collectors keep a register for this sort of information and the only danger in this is the possibility of it being parted from the collection and lost. Those that mark the album pages with costs don't really want the information openly displayed, so they use a code. A simple code would be to pick ten letters to equal one to ten; more sophisticated codes have letters standing for £25, £50, £100, etc. and use brackets for deductions, so if L equals £25 and P equals £5, a cost of £20 would be shown as L(P). The easiest way is to pick a word which does not have duplication of letters – otherwise it is easy to get mixed up with one's own code. Odd amounts can be shown in simple figures so an item costing £22 would be shown as L(3). A further refinement is to have capitals for pounds and lower case for pence. There are all sorts of codes which can be worked out.

It is a good idea to have a record of what was paid. When starting a collection it may not seem necessary, but it will prevent possible exploitation by an expert, particularly if your collection is inherited by someone who knows nothing of banknotes. It is also useful for those wishing to insure their collections.

5
The Evolution of Paper Money

Our knowledge of the earliest issues of paper money in the world is very limited. Paper as we know it today was invented circa AD200, but many collectors define paper money for collecting purposes as any piece of paper or substitute, such as leather, silk or cloth, used as money. There is evidence that during the Western Han Dynasty, Emperor Wu (140–86 BC) had white deer skins cut into pieces of one square foot each, embellished them with designs of water-plants and gave them a value of 400,000 copper coins. These are known as *Pai-lu-p'i-pi* and were probably the forerunner of paper money.

They did not circulate as money; visiting war-lords and dignitaries were required to purchase one and present it to the emperor in addition to their normal tribute. Failure to comply with the new Imperial custom was a beheading matter, so the deerskin money was promptly purchased.

China

The earliest mention of paper money as such is in about AD 650. Our sole reference for this and indeed for most of the early Chinese paper money is the book *Ch'uan Pu T'ung Chih* (*c.*1834) which took sixteen years to write and describes a total of 259 Chinese notes of which the author had acquired 221. He pictures a One Kwan note of the Emperor Yung Hui (AD 650–55), but states in the book that the first paper money to appear in China was between AD 806 and 820. It is possible that the AD 650 note was added near the completion of the book. The translator, Kojiro Tomita, tells us that the note is described as being issued by the Board of Revenue, but that the wording on the pictured note says 'Civil Board'. He points out that the characters for the two words are similar and that it was most probably a misprint. The author of *Ch'uan Pu T'ung Chih* clearly considered that he only had a few of the Chinese notes that had been issued in early times, for he states: 'As there are many hundreds of varieties of paper money, they could not be enumerated even on a hundred pages'.

Only a handful of the early Chinese notes are known at present, most of them in Chinese museums. The Museum of Fine Arts, Boston, has a set of photographs of the twenty notes of Chao-tsung, Lung-chi (AD 889–90) of the Tang Dynasty. The notes themselves have disappeared.

Notes of AD 800 which are known to have been preserved were called 'fei-chien' or 'flying money'. The advantage for merchants is obvious. Instead of having to cart wagon-loads of cash coins about the provinces at the mercy of bandits, a single horseman could ride out with the whole amount in paper and cash it at the point of destination. From the *Ch'uan Pu T'ung Chih* we learn that many of the early notes were coloured golden yellow or lake (the blue of lake water).

It is most improbable that modern collectors will be able to find any of these early notes. But notes of the Ming Dynasty, especially those issued at the commencement of the dynasty, AD 1368, do turn up and at auctions fetch anything from £200 to £1,000 according to condition. Collectors have a fascinating account by Marco Polo of the production of these giant notes from the skin below the bark of the mulberry tree.

The Ming notes were, apart from the inscriptions, the same as the Mongol notes, and also prepared from the mulberry tree. The Ming notes measure 32.5 × 22.5cm and are coloured dark slate. The inscriptions read 'Government of Ming Empire' and 'Government Note of the Ming Empire' circulating (under the Heavens) for Ever and Ever'. The borders are attractively designed with arabesque style flowers and dragons. In the centre is a pictorial representation of cash equal to the value of the note. These notes were not generally known to the West until the Boxer Rebellion in 1900. In the same manner that we put coins, etc., under foundation stones, the Chinese put items, including Ming notes, under statues of Buddha. During the looting of Peking, the Allied soldiers upturned a number of Buddha statues and found piles of notes under them. When one of these came up for sale in an American auction in 1900, it fetched $3,600. The price dropped fairly dramatically to $25 as more and more came to light.

Inflation destroyed the monetary value of the Ming notes, and by 1436 the government prohibited notes and returned to the cash coins. It would seem that for two hundred years there were no official Chinese issues of paper money. During the Ta Ching Dynasty the government found itself in difficulties. By 1651 they resorted to issuing paper money again, known as *Kuan Chao*, but these are scarcer than the Ming notes: it appears that the people did not trust them, recalling the days of the great inflations. The next paper money of China did not come about until 1854–9 with the advent of the T'ai Ping Rebellion. The Imperial Government issued Hsien Feng notes, the higher denominations nearly as large as the Ming notes; but these were now on white paper.

Paper money in Europe

The use of paper money in Europe can be traced back to the twelfth century, but these were not notes issued by banks and payable on demand. The true banknote did not appear in Europe until 1661, when Johan Palmstruch issued notes called *kreditivsedlar* on the Stockholms Banco to make up for a severe shortage of coin. The Chinese had been issuing such notes for centuries!

The need for banking facilities came about through international trade. Money-changers had to be extremely skilful and knowledgeable because of the innumerable gold and silver coins in circulation. The 'banchiere' of the Middle Ages worked from a bench in the street, using gold scales, touchstones and an abacus to value coins. Often the value of a coin was dependent on the actual town that minted it and the men most able to determine the good from the bad were the goldsmiths. It is often said that the goldsmiths were the fathers of modern banking; certainly they were the predominant money-changers of the Middle Ages. As their services became indispensable to the business community, they developed their business from that of an exchange banker to a deposit banker. A merchant would deposit coins or valuables and receive a written note declaring that a particular amount had been deposited. The population in those days was very small and both business and banking communities were well known to one another. Therefore the trader had no difficulty in surrendering his deposit note to another business man for goods; both knew the deposit banker and trusted him. The system became more refined when the banker would issue a receipt for the amount deposited in a fixed unit of account, based on precious metal which equalled the value of the items deposited with him. Letters of credit were issued to make foreign transactions easier, and before long ninety per cent of all trade was done in paper; the precious metals the paper represented were simply kept in the vaults of the banks or goldsmiths' store-rooms.

This meant that the merchants could trade freely with one another without the risk of being robbed and that the 'banks' were lending to each other. When one bank would find it owed a considerable amount to another after all the exchanges, they would fix an accounting date and ship out precious metal to that amount. A natural development from this was the bill of exchange. This bound one person to pay a specific amount to another person within a set period of time. It differed from a letter of credit in that it gave instructions to pay a particular person or company. Bills of exchange became the main medium of payment and circulated (with endorsements) in the same manner as modern banknotes. Some very early bills of exchange are known. On one occasion a Belgian historian examining the archives in Ypres came across some 8,000 bills of exchange dated between 1249 and 1291.

The banks became so powerful that kings found it convenient to borrow from them, on 'promise to pay' notes. The earliest recorded promise to pay of this type is dated 1199 and bears the signature of King John. It is made out to the merchants of Piacenza. In fact King John was repaying a debt of 2,125 silver marks lent by the merchants to Richard the Lionheart during the Holy Land crusades.

Although the goldsmiths formed the bulk of these early bankers there were others – including, strangely in view of the official attitude of forbidding the lending of money at interest, the Church. Monasteries were major lenders and for a time the Order of the Templars was the largest banking enterprise in Europe.

They were succeeded by the Lombards who by the fourteenth century had a virtual monopoly of banking. In England they had the monopoly at times, and to this day the street they operated from bears their name – Lombard Street in the City of London.

As the number of bankers grew, so did the failures. When a banker failed it meant that all the businessmen carrying his notes went down with him, or lost heavily. As a result of this a need grew for a safer form of banking; one controlled by the public. The first public bank was the Banco San Giorgio in Genoa which opened in 1407. It was not for some time that other cities caught on to the idea, but when the Genoa bank grew in stature other cities started public banks like the Banco di Rialto in Venice (1587) and the Wisselbank of Amsterdam in 1609.

From this developed the banking system that we have today. But it was not a new idea; such banking principles had been used in 2000 BC by the Babylonians, whose Temple Banks gave out letters of credit written on clay tablets which could be used at any of the temples associated with the issuer. At least one private bank, the Igibi bank in Sippari, was known to be making loans and receiving deposits circa 575 BC.

Collectors will find that there is often an association between a piece of paper money and the distant past when barter was the only form of exchange. A good example of this is the character 'Yuan' on Chinese banknotes (also, of course, the character 'Pao' on Chinese coins). In both these the foundation strokes are the word 'Pei' which means 'cowrie'. Cowries (seashells) have been used as money far longer than coins. They have been traced to the Shang Dynasty (1766–1122 BC) and, indeed, are still used in remote parts of the world.

Furs were used by the Russian people in ancient times as a means of exchange, and Dr E. Gribanov, the Soviet Union's leading authority on Russian paper money, has pointed out that the early names for metal coins were taken from the earlier fur 'coinage': belka (squirrel); shkura (hide), mordka (snout), ushki (little ears), and golovka (head).

Leather money was used on many occasions right up to modern times. It is claimed that leather currency existed in Sparta in 890 BC, but perhaps the most notable is the leather money of the Siege of Tyre in 1112, when the Doge Michieli paid his soldiers with it. The leather notes were stamped with the arms of his family and bore a promise to pay on the return of the fleet to Venice. Friedrich II, the German Emperor, used leather money to pay his troops at the Siege of Faenza in 1241 and had his portrait put on the leather with silver thread.

The last appearance of leather money was in the 1920s when some now rare German notgeld known as 'heel and toe' notgeld was issued. They were leather notes which could quite literally be used to repair shoes. As inflation carried away the value of the notes, these heel and toe notes went up in value way above their face value in line with the cost of shoe repairs.

Paper money was basically introduced in cases of emergency and this is one of the reasons why it is so popular among collectors. Most of the early notes of the world have a fascinating history behind them. In Norway, for example, Jorgen Thor Mohlen issued paper money in 1695. He got permission from the King in an attempt to avoid a calamity, when he began losing ships to pirates. He was the richest man in Norway, with factories producing everything from rope to gunpowder and a large part of the population depended on him. His credit was seriously affected by pirate losses and Mohlen asked the King to let him issue notes until his trading ships returned. He was authorised to issue 50,000 krondaler with the wording 'As His Royal Majesty the 22 June this year 1695 / his most gracious Decree has issued/ regarding certain Notes/ that shall go for Money North of the Mountains in His Royal Majesty's Kingdom, Norway/ Then is this Note according to the said Decree authorised for the value of... Rixdale/Croner'. Unfortunately for Mohlen the people did not trust the notes and presented them for payment the moment they got them. Mohlen was forced into bankruptcy and was to die a poor man in 1709.

The United States

The development of paper money in the United States started when the Red Indians were still a major force to be reckoned with. The early Colonial issues were all made for purposes of war. The first, made in Massachusetts Bay in 1690, was to pay for the military expedition to Canada, known as King William's War, in 1689–97. A few years later South Carolina issued notes to pay for the military expedition against the Spanish and Indians in Florida. During Queen Anne's War (1702–13), New Hampshire, Connecticut, New York and New Jersey all issued notes.

Although the inhabitants would have liked to have paper money, as coin was so scarce, the British Governors were

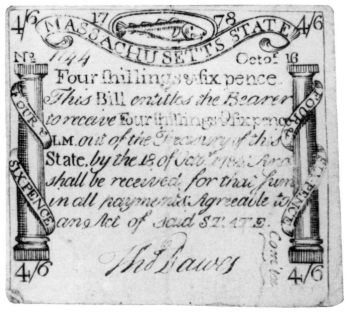

1 Early note for 4*s*.6*d*. issued in Massachusetts in 1778, known to collectors as the 'Codfish' note, because of the fish design engraved by Paul Revere.

instructed by their Government not to permit paper money issues except in cases of military emergency. Some States ignored these regulations and went ahead and issued paper money.

With the coming of the War of Independence, the Americans issued masses of paper money to pay for the war. Some of these notes refer specifically to the war '. . . at or before the End of one Year after the Expiration of the present war, or a Cessation of Hostilities between Great Britain and these United States . . .'. Paper money was soon used for propaganda purposes and shows George III trampling on the Magna Carta and burning American towns. One of history's famous figures, Paul Revere, engraved and printed notes showing a Minute Man with sword in hand and the words: 'Issued in defence of American Liberty' (**1**). Benjamin Franklin invented the marble-paper used for some notes and printed notes which bear his name as the printer.

2 $8 Continental Congress note of 1778. These notes became valueless and led to the expression 'not worth a Continental'.

The Continental Congress issued its own notes. At first, when a final break with England was not being seriously considered, the title on the notes was 'The United Colonies', but in 1777 the title ominously changed to 'United States'. Certain States, like Maryland, had used the Spanish dollar for their denominations, but now all the States changed over from sterling to Spanish dollars to make the break with England more final (**2**). The very early cheques of the United States are often found with the dollar equalling 90 cents, e.g. 'Five Dollars and 20/90 cents'. This was because of the Spanish milled dollar.

Collectors who like history will find the early American notes a superb field for examination (**3**). All of them are handsigned by prominent citizens so that the public would accept them, and these include nine who signed the Declaration of Independence, ten Delegates to the Stamp Act Congress and eleven signatories to the United States Constitution.

It is interesting that as far back as 1828 a serious collector of these issues existed, a man called Joshua I. Cohen. William

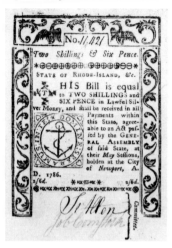

3 2s.6d. note of Rhode Island issued in 1786. The legal tender provision was to be enforced without the right of trial by jury, and became the subject of a court case, Trevett *v.* Weeden. It was ruled invalid because it denied trial by jury and so these notes established the common law principle of trial by jury as a fundamental right of citizens of the USA.

Bentley refers to the colonial notes in his diary in 1787, and George Washington himself kept a sheet of Continental Currency as a souvenir.

Playing cards were used as money in Canada in 1685. Jacques de Meulles, Intendant of New France, unable to pay his troops in coin, had the idea of using playing cards instead. The date and denomination were written on the back and the cards were then signed by the Governor and the Intendant and countersigned by the Clerk of the Treasury as they were issued.

The cards were cut to different sizes in line with the denominations. It seems that the authorities were aware of the dangers of over-issue of paper money and from the start it was an offence punishable by death to retain the playing card money after the redemption date. That is one reason why these issues are so exceptionally scarce today. There are sixteen different examples of this money in the Bank of Canada Collection. When the battle of Quebec put an end to French sovereignty over

Canada the French Government refused to honour the outstanding notes. Finally the British Government authorised money to redeem the notes at twenty-five per cent of face.

Australia

Australia was inhabited by aborigines alone until the nineteenth century. It was Captain James Cook's famous voyages to the South Seas (1768–71) during which he explored the east coast of Australia, which first attracted the idea of a settlement. On board was a rich young amateur naturalist, to become Sir Joseph Banks. He had taken with him a group of artists and topographers to make drawings of the flora and fauna, etc. of each place visited. Captain Cook made a landing at what is now 'Botany Bay' to allow Banks and his fellow naturalist Solander to make their investigations.

At that time Britain's unemployment was roughly one in nine and the crime rate was soaring. It was the practice to transport convicts to America but the War of Independence put an end to that practice. A Committee was set up to examine the whole question of housing convicts, and Sir Joseph Banks gave evidence before the Committee, recommending Botany Bay.

The first governor of the new settlement was Captain Arthur Phillip, Royal Navy, who sailed in HMS *Sirius* with ten other ships on 13 May 1787. He landed at Botany Bay, but soon found that while it might have been fine for natural history, it was not suitable for a convict settlement, and moved to Sydney Cove, where the Union Jack was unfurled on 26 January 1788, celebrated ever since as Australia Day. Nearly 1,500 people landed, including 759 convicts. Before transportation ended, over 150,000 convicts were transported to Australia.

What little coin there was did not suffice for everyone's need and was mainly used for paying for imported goods. For a long time barter was the only recourse left to the small population. Rum became the main currency of Australia and was in use well into the nineteenth century. Even the Government used barter items and early posters offered flour as a reward for information. The judge of an assault case ordered compensation to be paid in the form of a gallon of rum. A gallon of rum was worth thirty shillings in those days, and as importers were often paying as little as 1s.6d. a gallon there were huge profits to be made. As one importer wrote: 'For a goat I should pay in money £10 sterling, but for less than eight gallons of spirits, at 18d. the gallon, I can make the same purchase'.

When Governor King took over the colony he decided that the effects of a Rum currency were not good for the colony, and he tried to ban spirits altogether. Although he did not succeed, he turned away ships carrying over 100,000 gallons of spirits and wines during his term of office. This created havoc with the currency system and the population resorted to paper money. It was the next best thing to heaven for the convicts who suddenly found they could write out their own 'banknotes'. Some of them, practised in the art of forgery, obtained letters from well-known people and cut the signature area off the letter, adding to it an 'I promise to pay . . .' which was readily accepted.

Very soon Governor King was not at all happy about paper money either. He issued a proclamation permitting the settlement of debts in pig meat. The value of swine flesh was fixed at 7d. a pound. In 1880 he also introduced specially printed forms, available from 24 October of that year for use as promissory notes, by those people whom he personally approved. It appears that very few people took any notice, though they happily used the printed forms as well, if they could get his approval.

The earliest notes were store receipts issued by military authorities and intended to be presented to the Commissary General for payment. In fact they often circulated from hand to hand for many months before redemption. In charge of the printed form notes was Garnham Blaxcell, whose notes of around 1814 are among the earliest notes available to collectors. He had started out as a purser's assistant in the Royal Navy before becoming Governor King's secretary. With two other merchants he agreed to build Sydney Hospital at no cost to the colony. Governor Macquarie was criticised for this charitable act because he let them have a monopoly of the importation of rum – still a major currency – in return. The hospital, which opened in July 1817, was known locally as 'Rum Hospital'.

A great many people and firms were soon issuing notes despite legislation to prevent them. These gradually developed into fully printed notes (**4**), some in sterling, and some in Spanish dollars. One of the early nineteenth-century printed notes, which

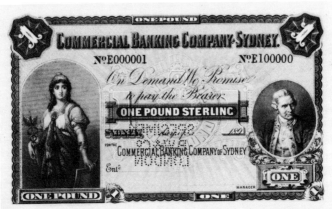

4 Early Australian notes of the nineteenth century were among the first to be beautifully engraved. (**a**) £100 Commercial Bank note with oriental characters to facilitate the influx of foreign labour in Sydney; (**b**) £1 Commercial Banking Company note, picturing Captain Cook on the right.

features a kangaroo, was issued by a prominent Jewish property owner, Emanuel Solomon of Adelaide, who was later elected to the Legislative Council in South Australia. Mining companies, hotels and vineyards were soon issuing their own notes. Very often the issuers made sure that the notes were printed on inferior paper in the hope that they would deteriorate before they could be cashed. These notes were soon called 'shinplasters' and it is recorded that one publican would put his notes in the oven to make them brittle and hasten their deterioration. Collectors need to be careful of facsimiles produced by White Wings Ltd. for inclusion in their packs of 'Kool Pops' (ready to freeze water ice block mixes). They are easy to identify as they are printed on coloured paper. Genuine notes were generally printed on white paper and are usually larger.

India

One form of paper money peculiar to India is the Hundi. It covers a whole range of monetary transactions with types of Hundi payable on demand, payable on fixed dates, after a specified time, and so on.

For centuries they were the most common form of currency in India and their ancestry goes back long before the invention of paper. Some authorities, like Narendra S. Sengar, trace their use back nearly three thousand years, pre-dating the earliest known Chinese banknotes, though of course the Hundi is not a banknote as such; merely serving the same purpose. The Hundi had a religious significance which more than anything else gave it a better chance of being honoured. The bankers who issued them were known as shroffs and sahukars in India, and use a cursive Indian script long since out of general use, and making it hard to understand even for Indian students.

The British East India Co., found the Hundi so well established that rather than try and replace it, they adopted it and appointed a banker specially to handle Hundi transactions for them. In 1860 the British introduced a tax of approximately one anna for every 100 rupees transacted by Hundi. It was a very lucrative source of income, and in 1881 the Government printed Hundis with the portrait of Queen Victoria. There is a maze of different Hundis because all the Princely States issued their own.

During Muslim rule in India the Hundi suffered because the penalties for even witnessing a Hundi transaction were eternal damnation. Various sorts of Hundis were issued, some 'to be paid to an honourable person only', some not negotiable and payable only to the named person, others to be paid on a fixed date or after a specified time, and those negotiable by endorsement. When the British increased the tax in 1910, not all the Princely States followed suit, so that a Hundi issued in a State, but sent for redemption to British India, had to have additional tax stamps (adhesive) applied to it. In 1955 another form of Hundi was introduced, printed just like normal banknotes. These were issued by the All India Khadi and Village Industries Board and could only be used to purchase Khadi, which is a type of handspun and handwoven cloth.

There is a great deal of research needed into Hundis and it is an interesting and inexpensive field of study. Often one can find Hundis on sale for as little as 50p, mainly because the vendor cannot distinguish them from the more common, but similar, legal documents.

The first serious attempt to catalogue the main issues is found in *The Standard Guide to South Asian Coins and Paper Money*, published by Krause Publications, which devotes nearly thirty pages to the subject.

6

Inflation Notes

Germany

Among the first notes to come to the attention of new collectors are the often colourful and varied issues of the German hyper-inflation period. Many of these notes can still be obtained in perfect condition for as little as £1. The story behind them is quite fascinating. When the signs of inflation began to show, the German mark was worth 38 to the pound and 7.95 to the dollar. That was in January 1919, and by September the mark had reached 100 to the pound. At the beginning of 1920, it was 188.50 marks to the pound, and it went up to 351 on 9 March, before falling back again. During 1921 it climbed, and broke the thousand barrier on 7 November. The general population were beginning to grumble about inflation – but they were going to get a worse inflation than they could imagine. Throughout 1922 the rate went up and up with slight fluctuations, reaching 34,250 marks to the pound in December (**5**).

On 17 July 1923, the pound was worth a million marks and the flood-gates were open. By October, the pound was worth 58,500,000 marks, and on 1 November it reached 600 milliarden (1,000 million marks equalled 1 milliarde) (**6**). On some days the inflation rate actually doubled. 14 November saw 5,500 milliarden to the pound, and the next day it was 11,000 milliarden. The inflation reached its peak in April 1924 at 18,500 milliarden to the pound.

Hundreds of different types of notes were issued during this period, rising in denomination to 100 billion marks – worth less than £7 at the time of issue. But many notes with dates as early as 1908 and 1910 were caught up in the inflationary spiral. More and more were printed before the government resorted to higher denominations.

Towards the end of World War I, it was common knowledge in Germany that the war was lost. The value of the mark fell and,

5 German inflation note for 10,000 marks, issued in 1922. If you turn the note to the left and put your thumb over the young man's face, a vampire appears. This represents the viciousness of the Versailles treaty, bleeding young Germany dry.

correspondingly, the price of goods increased. It became necessary to print more notes, but at this time the German Printing Works were hit by a strike. The Government was embarrassed because it had only just issued a prohibition order on the emergency issues, German notgeld, which had been issued by just about every town and city in Germany, and even by firms, shops and police stations. The Reichsbank could not cope with the situation and the Government had to invite cities and large concerns to issue their own notes again.

The final blow to any regulation of German finance was the occupation of the Rhine and Ruhr areas by French and Belgian troops – the very heart of industrial Germany. The citizens responded with a General Strike and the Berlin Government had to pay relief for the millions of workers. The only possible way of doing this was to print more notes.

6 German inflation note for one billion marks issued 1 November 1923, when 600 milliarden equalled one pound.

Everything became chaotic and merchants found themselves re-pricing goods twice in a day. An employee who had worked a full week and then received his wages, saw them depreciate to half their value the next day. Industries began paying wages twice a week, and finally every day.

Because the Reichsbank could not keep up with the printing needs, they began to overprint older, obsolete issues with higher denominations. One issue, Kreis Rastenburg, was overprinted twice on the same note. The Reichsbank printers had to call in private printing companies to help. In fact, eighty-four private companies, with sixty more assisting in some way or another, were used to print notes: 30,000 people worked on the printing of banknotes for the State; and no-one knows how many were employed on local issues. Thirty different types of paper were used and 400,000 printing plates were provided by the Central Office to the various printing houses.

However, this German inflation was by no means the worst ever known. Indeed, there had been inflations of similar magnitude as far back as the Yuan (or Mongol) Dynasty of China (see chapter 5).

John Law and the French assignat

The French Revolution was another inflation that rocked a nation – almost as much as the guillotine – when the French assignat came into being. It was the brainchild of a Scotsman, John Law, though they were not actually issued until seventy years after his death. But Law was responsible for a major inflation in his time, and gave the world the word 'millionaire'.

John Law was a financier who strongly opposed the current merchant theory that a nation's wealth was its stock of precious metals, and contended that gold and silver fluctuated like corn, whereas land was steady in value, intrinsically useful and always in demand. Paper money would be secured by mortgages to the value of two-thirds of the land value, or issued for the entire amount if the land was turned over to the Commission. His theory was that currency would regulate itself, because the currency could be in proportion to the needs of the community. If a man wanted money and had land to secure it, he could get it; when no one needed money, there would be no demand and none would be issued. The canny Scots turned this idea down flat, but later Law met the Duke of Orleans, who was so impressed with Law's mathematical abilities that when he became Regent of France, he turned to Law for assistance in solving France's financial problems.

This time Law was advancing a theory of money created on the security of commercial credit. He was granted a charter for a private bank, and in 1716 the 'Banque Générale' opened quietly in the house where he lived, Place Louis le Grand. His notes were redeemable in coin of a fixed weight, which brought immediate success, as it meant they could not be devalued by royal edict, a common enough occurrence, and it enabled business relations to open abroad.

Within two years his bank became a State Bank, and then he moved to financial heights which were to dazzle the world. He produced his scheme for the Mississippi Company, the *Compagnie d'Occident*, which was to enjoy extensive and monopolistic privileges in Louisiana. His next proposal was nothing less than the conversion of the national debt. He offered to advance the State 1,500 million livres at three per cent, intending to raise the money by company shares. In one audacious move to attract investors he took an option on shares of the company himself, at a price 200 livres above the market, and deposited 40,000 livres as security. Investors rushed in to buy. In July 1719, shares issued at 500 livres were quoted at 1,000, and two months later the same

49

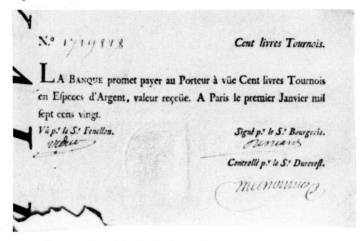

7 100 livre note from John Law's 'Banque Royale', dated 1720. It had started as the 'Banque Générale' in a private house, but the name was changed when it became the national bank.

---

shares were up to 5,000. To stop an incipient run on the bank Law lowered the value of gold! He substantially increased the value of paper money by lowering the redemption rate to thirty-four livres paper to the louis.

The consequences of this had no parallel in previous history. The Rue Quincampoix drew speculators from every part of Europe. Speculators who bought in October 1719 made a hundred per cent profit a month later. Fortunes were not the prerogative of the financial men; a bootblack made forty million, a waiter thirty million. The word 'millionaire' was used to describe the Mississippian who had suddenly become wealthy (7).

When John Law visited the Rue Quincampoix where the deals were made, he was treated like royalty. Edinburgh, overlooking his past history, sent him the Freedom of the City. France rewarded him with the highest position in the financial world, Comptroller General. It could not last long, and did not. When large stocks were placed on the market, panic followed, and Law's empire crumbled around him. On 10 October 1720, a decree was issued formally declaring the notes of the bank no longer currency. John Law fled the country.

Many years later, in 1789, his theory of land money was translated into French. The Revolutionary National Assembly had just confiscated the property of the Church and were positively eager to implement the theory of land money. It is perhaps surprising that they did not heed the experience of their own history of note-issuing.

The French Revolution

The French Revolution lasted for ten years, from 1789 to 1799, and began with the rural disturbances in the summer of 1789 which led to the fall of the Bastille and decrees abolishing feudal rights and privileges. The Convention abolished the Monarchy and cut off the head of King Louis XVI. But the real violence did not come until the radical Jacobins gained control of the Convention from the moderate Girondists and instituted the notorious Reign of Terror. The fall of Robespierre in July 1794 saw a more moderate government, which in its turn was finally overthrown by Napoleon Bonaparte in 1799.

The National Assembly created the 'Caisse de l'Extraordinaire' which issued the assignats and the first issue of 16/17 April 1790 had interest-bearing coupons and were for high denominations of 200, 300 and 1,000 livres. It has been argued fairly convincingly by some monetarists that the scheme was sound enough and at this time showed every sign of succeeding. It was over-issue, rather than the idea, which caused inflation.

These high denominations had little effect on the working population, whose average wage was twenty-five sous a day. These assignats were intended to increase the money supply so that the lands, the 'Domaines Nationaux' could be purchased: unsold they had little use to the revolutionaries.

Subsequent issues were made which were not interest-bearing and denominations began to appear for 50, 60, 70, 80 and so on, up to 2,000 livres. But even the smallest denomination, the 50 livres, was only available to fairly wealthy businessmen and the shortage of small money led to organisations and towns issuing 'billets de confiance', of which many hundreds exist. To

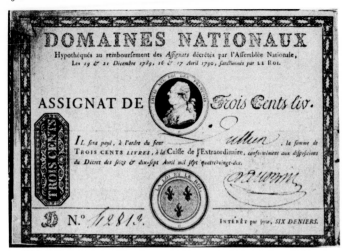

8 A Face Royale of the French Revolution for 300 livres. The King was recognised from the portrait on one of these notes when he tried to escape from Paris in 1791.

overcome this the National Assembly ordered an issue of five livre assignats on 6 May 1791, entitled 'Domaines Nationaux'. The early assignats are testimony to the fact that the revolutionaries did not at first contemplate the destruction of the monarchy. They bore the portrait of the King and are known to collectors as 'Face Royales' (**8**). It is said that the King was recognised from the portrait on one of these notes when he tried to escape from Paris in 1791. The last Face Royale, a twenty-five livre note, was issued on 16 December 1791. Indeed, up until 24 October 1792 many of the notes bear the inscription 'La Loi et Le Roi' (The Law and the King). Then came the September Convention, and a sudden change in style with Republican symbols of fasces, liberty caps, etc. (**9**).

Over-issue of assignats began to take its toll. By March 1792 they were worth about forty-two per cent of their face value. Against this, a loaf of bread had been three sous, but by May 1793 was costing twelve sous. Food scarcity forced prices up even further and the rapidly climbing inflation was only temporarily halted by new laws on maximum prices introduced in May 1793.

9 Assignat of the French Revolution, still common today. They fetch on average £3 to £5 each in perfect condition, and not infrequently turn up in uncut sheets.

With the Reign of Terror, which started in July 1793, Robespierre was able to bring a little stability to the assignat. The Committees of Public Safety and General Security sent to the guillotine anyone suspected of hoarding, counterfeiting or speculating in the nation's currency. However, as more and more assignats were issued, the value continued to depreciate, until it reached approximately a quarter of one per cent of face value. Confidence in paper money was gone and the Directory Government took what has now become a standard step, the introduction of a new unit of currency. They replaced the livre with the franc, and issued notes for 100, 750, 1,000, 2,000 and 10,000 francs. If anything, the value depreciated even faster than that of the livre had done. The Government assured the people that all would be well and a great fuss was made about the new type of currency which was planned to replace the assignat system. All the plates, stocks of assignats and even the tools used to make them, were publicly and ceremonially burned in the Place Vendôme.

The cure was to be the 'Promesses de Mandats Territoriaux', which were issued under the decree of 28 Ventose An IV (18

53

March 1796). An exchange rate was given to assignats of thirty to one, but within months inflation was back in full force with some eighty-two billion livres of assignat value in circulation. In fact the cure came from an unexpected source. Napoleon was waging very successful military campaigns and the plunder of war was beginning to arrive in Paris – in the year V of the Revolution, thirty-six tons of gold bullion arrived at the Paris Mint. Still the Government continued issuing paper money, but this time in a very unusual form, lottery 'billets'. They were valid as currency and carried with them the opportunity of winning twelve million francs. They did, however, have the disadvantage of becoming worthless after the draw and they were not well received by the public.

No-one had any confidence in government issues any more and it was left to a few private banks to issue notes until the establishment of the Bank of France under Napoleon. Napoleon held firm to his promise to the people: 'While I live, I will never resort to irredeemable paper'.

Hungary

All these inflations paled in the light of the Hungarian inflation after World War II. The Hungarian economy collapsed in the bleak winter opening of 1945. Banknote issues of the National Bank of Hungary came to a stop because the Arrow Cross (the Hungarian Nazi supporters) took all the gold which backed the banknotes. At the same time the Red Army overran the country. Taxation and rationing systems broke down. F. Winkle, the economist, described the position: 'The maintenance of foreign occupation troops means a further incomputable burden, not to mention reparation payments, which had to start as soon as the Soviet armies were in full occupation, when conditions were most chaotic. Confusion was also created by the occupation forces issuing pengo notes of their own. The main factor, however, was the ever-growing State deficit.

'With production at a standstill, a considerable portion of the country's working population abroad in concentration and prisoner of war camps, faced by enormous destruction and political uncertainty, it is not surprising that taxes remained unpaid. There were no funds to pay for salaries, for the most immediate and urgent reconstruction, for reparations or for the maintenance of occupation armies. These were the real causes which forced the Government to resort to the most unjust means of taxation – that of inflation.'

By the autumn of 1945, the pengo was depreciating in value at an alarming rate. The Government decided that the cure was to cut the amount of money in circulation, as it was thought that this would lead to a fall in prices. A Decree Law was passed in December 1945 stating that all notes of 1,000 pengo or more were prohibited from further circulation unless special tax stamps were affixed to them. These stamps could only be purchased from the Government at a cost of three times the face value of the note. The system had the logic of getting in revenue for the Government whose tax collecting system had broken down. It meant that a quarter of the circulating currency notes would remain in circulation. The holder of a 1,000 pengo note had to pay 3,000 pengos to the State in order to be able to use his 1,000 pengo note. Inflation, it was thought, would soon come under control, but the authorities had overlooked bank accounts. People could write cheques for goods and avoid the tax-stamps, and so inflation increased.

In the first month of 1946 the Hungarian Government introduced the tax-pengo (adopengo) which was a theoretical unit based on the price index. Taxes, levied in tax-pengo, would be payable in paper pengo at the ruling rate which was fixed daily. While originally the tax pengo was intended purely for use for tax purposes, it was soon being used for private transactions. It benefitted bank customers, as they could deposit money one day, which would be given a tax-pengo valuation, and draw it out the next day in much larger quantity, due to the revaluation of their accounts calculated in tax-pengos.

In June 1946 tax-pengo notes were issued. They could be obtained by exchanging normal pengo notes at post offices or banks. The note-holder could now hold them without worrying about inflation, and when used, the value would be calculated in regular pengo corresponding to the rate of the tax pengo of that day.

Before the pengo notes became virtually valueless they went through a series of multiple unit changes, which better than anything give collectors an idea of how rampant the inflation

10 Hungarian inflation note for 10 million milpengo, issued in 1946 and showing Lajos Kossuth, the great Hungarian patriot and freedom fighter.

---

was. The first was a new multiple unit of the milpengo (equal to a million pengos) (**10**); and just three months later this was replaced by the bilpengo (equal to a billion pengos). Hungary produced the highest face value note the world has ever seen with its one hundred million bilpengo. In fact the Government prepared another unit, the billion bilpengo, but it was never issued. A billion bilpengos equalled a 1 followed by 28 zeros. For the ordinary citizen it became a nightmare. Trillions, quadrillions and quintillions meant nothing. They ceased to use figures for daily purchases and spoke in terms of the tax-pengos whose pengo value altered daily as 'two blues and a red' when making a deal. Collectors should not overlook the fact that during this period tax-accounting letters of credit, law courts fees and deed stamps were officially declared legal tender. The forint replaced the pengo, and was legally defined as a gold currency in 1946. The ratio of conversion was quite staggering: 200 million tax-pengos equalled one forint. This meant that it took 400,000 billion in bilpengoes, 400,000 trillion in mil-pengos and 400,000 quadrillion in pengos to secure one forint.

Greece

Perhaps the most devastating inflation in modern times was the Greek inflation of World War II. This was not a case of the financial affairs of a country getting out of hand. It was a cold-blooded deliberate policy of destroying an economy. The Germans, having conquered Greece, decided to ruin the economy and they succeeded.

The Germans had not contemplated an attack against Greece so early in the war, but their ebullient allies the Italians under Mussolini could not wait to get in on the act, and the Duce proudly informed Hitler that his armies were marching. On the eve of the big Italian offensive against Greece, the country had 12,598,979,600 drachmae in circulation. It was a well regulated currency. The Greeks did not take kindly to the Italian invasion and promptly blooded Mussolini's nose. By 6 April the following year, despite the problems of being invaded, Greece had controlled its finances comparatively well and the increase in circulating drachmae had only risen to 19,371,436,350 drachmae.

Hitler could hardly permit his Italian allies to suffer such degradation and on that day the German army crossed the frontiers to aid the Italians. It was soon all over. The Germans then set about systematically draining Greece of all its valuables, which were sent by train-loads to the Reich, and gave them paper money instead. Before the Germans retreated towards the end of the war they had in circulation the quite fantastic figure of 6,500,000,000,000,000,000 drachmae.

The Institute of Mining Credit in Greece published a booklet straight after the war which is in itself a collector's item as it contains twenty-five inflation drachmae. The first page (printed in both Greek and English) states: 'For us Greeks and the succeeding generations, a collection of the bank notes and paper money put into circulation in Greece by the Germans and Italians during the occupation, will be a horrible nightmare and an unshakeable proof of the afflictions that our old and historical country has gone through. The Institute of Mining Credit compiled this collection as a symbol of a heroic epoch in Greece's history which vies with older epochs for excellence.'

The booklet calculated the damage to Greece's economy as exceeding 325 million sovereigns. In pre-war drachmae this represented 118 billion drachmae. Some 700 ships were lost, only one port remained serviceable, four-fifths of the road system was destroyed and of 220 railway engines, only 15 remained.

11 Greek inflation note for 5 million drachmas, dated 20 July 1944, showing Arethusa on a dekadrachm of Syracuse.

On 9 November 1944 the Greek Government was again in control of its own affairs. New drachmae were issued with an exchange rate of one for 50,000 million inflation drachmae. The booklet states: 'Thus we find that, when after four hundred years of subjugation to the Turks she regained her freedom, the first 10 lepta coin issued in 1828 by the Capodistrian Government bore on it the Phoenix as an emblem. And now after four dark years of occupation, the first drachma to be issued by the government of Liberation bears on it again, the Phoenix.' Many of the Greek inflation notes depict rare coins of Ancient Greece(**11**) and make an interesting collection.

Russia

While Russia evaded inflationary issues of banknotes during World War II – simply by letting everyone go without – inflation hit the nation during the Russian revolution which followed World War I. Historically Russia had always been conservative with its note issues, and for most of its early history a hundred rouble note was the highest denomination issued. From 1819 to 1843 some 200 rouble notes were printed, and in the late nineteenth century high denominations of 500 and 1,000 roubles were prepared, but never issued. In 1912 a giant-sized 500 rouble note picturing Peter the Great made its appearance.

This was the highest denomination in circulation at the time of the Russian Revolution. The currency had been kept down by Nicholas II, the last of the Czars, who issued a moratorium freezing all bank accounts of over 100 roubles. Account holders were only permitted to withdraw five per cent of the balance of their accounts each month. At that time 2,431 million roubles were in circulation.

Care is needed by collectors in identifying some of the magnificent notes of this period because, long after his death, the notes of the Czar continued to be printed, and they can only be distinguished by signatures and serial prefixes. The 500 rouble note bore the signature of A. Konshin when it was first issued, but when reissued from 1912 to 1917, they had the signature of I. Shipov. Some of the Shipov notes are difficult to identify when they have been printed by the Provisional Government and also by the Soviet Government, but generally they possess lighter colours than the originals printed during the Czarist period.

A maze of notes began to be issued when the Revolution broke out. Notes for North Russia were actually printed in England and backed by Barclays Bank to support the Chaikovskii Government. As inflation began to take hold, Barclays became nervous enough to 'block out' the printed paragraph on the note which referred to redemption in gold in London!

The short-lived Kerensky Government found that the local printing presses could not produce enough new money for their needs. Also, the note printing was of such poor quality that people often refused to accept them. Kerensky was producing 800 million roubles a month, but it was still not enough. Contracts were made with the American Bank Note Company, but when a shipload of these beautifully engraved and printed notes arrived, they were too late. The Kerensky Government had collapsed and for a long time the notes lay idle in the hold of the ship. Small change was also a problem as all silver coins had been hoarded. Small treasury notes totalling 1,000 million roubles were issued and nicknamed 'beer stamps' in Russia. These were not enough, and the Government resorted to printing postage stamps on thicker than normal paper and overprinting them as currency.

From a collecting point of view the Russian Revolution offers a variety of historically interesting and colourful notes which often repay research. Very little is known about some issues, but unusual and extremely rare items can be found, for example notes issued by the British Military Mission, and the YMCA. Inflation was rampant, paper money always seemed to be in short supply, and by the end of 1920 it took 13,000 roubles to buy what one rouble would have bought in 1913.

The 'Interventionists', i.e. foreign troops fresh from the battle-fields of World War I, were soon issuing their own paper money. Through this paper money collectors can piece together the history of the struggle which set the pace for modern politics and the East versus West position that exists today. It was difficult to see how such a magnificently-honed fighting force could possibly lose to Russia, still recoiling from the effects of World War I, and in the throes of revolution. Following the German surrender, the Red Army reconquered the Baltic States, Poland and the Ukraine. The Versailles statesmen, particularly President Wilson, who wanted to redraw the map of Europe on the basis of national self-determination, were furious. They did not foresee the East *v.* West confrontation ahead at that time. France wanted Poland to be strong enough always to be a threat to Germany; the British were concerned with the future of Asiatic Russia, and wanted security for India which could only be gained by setting up a puppet regime in Central Asia. Japan wanted Eastern Siberia, and the Romanians wanted to keep Bessarabia. So the Allies went in with force of arms.

Had the 'Interventionists' been united, the results might have been different, but the British had no wish to help France create a great Poland; France was not interested in Britain's buffer state in Central Asia, and America was quite definitely hostile to the Japanese desire for part of Siberia. The amount of help the Great Powers were prepared to put into intervention was therefore limited. The men, fed up with the long bitter struggle of World War I, wanted to go home. Indeed the French army sent to Odessa in 1919 had to be withdrawn because of its disturbing tendency to shoot its officers.

The hope of the Interventionists lay with Admiral Kolchak, distinguished naval commander, a man of known courage and honesty, and a famous Arctic explorer. The British, in particular, encouraged him to seize power and British troops under Colonel Ward supported him as he led a colourful and much romanticised charge of the famous Cossacks to take Ormsk and establish the 'Provisional Russian Government'.

When Admiral Kolchak moved on Moscow, he expected Generals Denikin and Wrangel, commanding equally large forces, to assist in a pincer movement. But they failed to assist, the Red Army counter-attacked, and Kolchak's Government head-quarters at Ormsk, guarded by the Middlesex Regiment, had to move out. By the time Kolchak's forces reached Irkutsk they were little more than a rabble. The victorious Red Army ordered Admiral Kolchak to be executed and the Czech Army were happy to oblige. At the age of forty-six, Kolchak found himself under the guard of his own men and, on 7 February 1920, faced a firing squad.

Kolchak had little difficulty in getting his paper money accepted. He controlled the Trans-Siberian railway – at least the Czechs nominally under his command did – and he had care of the National Gold Reserve of Russia which was contained in twenty-nine heavily guarded freight trucks. He issued a maze of notes for the Provisional Russian Government. English and French languages are found on the notes as well as Russian so that his troops could understand enough to use them. There were nine different dated issues of these notes and the 5,000 rouble notes, clearly intended to impress, were over a foot long.

But the Kolchak government still could not provide enough paper money for its needs. They solved the problem, partly, by making use of the American printed notes which still lay in the hold of a ship in Vladivostok and which had been intended for the Kerensky government, but had arrived too late. Among the paper money were $4\frac{1}{2}$ per cent Government bonds. Kolchak had them put into circulation as banknotes. The bonds were to represent their face value of 200 roubles and the coupons (there were 20 to each bond) were to act as small change notes for 4.50 roubles each. Later many of these were to remain in circulation with the overprint 'Siberian Revolutionary Committee'.

The banknotes in the cargo were beautifully engraved and colourful – the work of the American Banknote Company. These notes, apart from the fractionals, have an allegorical seated woman forming the centre vignette. The main issue was made by Kolchak but notes from the same ship-load found their way to other areas. Some were used by the Provisional Power of the Pribaikal Region and were issued in 1920. Although without signature, as with some of the earlier issues, they have a red overprint of the Russian double-eagle on the reverse. A year later, in 1921, the same notes appear for the Far Eastern Republic and are easily recognised by the bronze circular overprint on the reverse.

The American Bank Note Company were not at all pleased to find their notes, printed for Kerensky, being used by just about everyone else, including the communists. It was one of the few occasions when they allowed the banknote designs to be used by another country – the vignette was to appear on notes of Ecuador at a later date.

Many of the powerful generals took it on themselves to issue notes. General Denikin, General Wrangel and General Yudenitch have all left behind various types of paper money. Some were issued by private armies and such people as the self-styled 'Prince Avolloff', who was in fact a Colonel. Notes of the Czarist period and Provisional Government were revalidated by perforation and issued again to help ease the shortage of paper money.

One reason why so much paper money of the Russian revolutionary period is still found today is that the Russian nobility fled to the West bringing it with them, in suitcases. However, the Socialistic Federation of Soviets of Russia made invalid all those notes taken to the West, and so caused many wealthy families to become paupers overnight.

During the revolution over 10,000 different notes were issued. Some of the regions suffered worse inflations than others. The Transcaucasia started out with one, three and five rouble notes in 1918, but by 1924 had denominations of 10,000 million roubles. They issued many denominations in millions and were the only territory in the world to issue a 75 million denomination.

China

China did not escape inflation in World War II. The Central Bank of China introduced an unusual currency in the form of Customs Gold Units in 1930. This was the idea of Professor Edwin Kemmer and it was intended that they should be used for paying customs import duties. But by the end of World War II inflation had overtaken these notes and they were being used in normal circulation, but with ever decreasing value and higher

12 One million gold yuan issued in 1949 by the Central Bank of China, depicting General Chiang Kai-Shek, whose lost cause against communism led to an enormous inflation.

denominations. They started in 1930 with modest denominations of ten and twenty cents, but by 1947 they had reached 10,000 CGU and in 1948 they reached 250,000 CGU.

The situation was getting out of hand and the Kuo Min Tang Government responded on 19 August 1948 by introducing a completely new unit, the Gold Yuan. It was to be backed by forty per cent gold and sixty per cent securities. The population were told that no notes of over 100 Gold Yuan would be issued and that the total issue would not exceed two billion dollars worth. But this was soon forgotten. The Gold Yuan was equal to $3 million CGU but the new notes were soon reaching denominations of 5 million and bore the portrait of Chiang-Kai-Shek (**12**). Even this was not enough and the bank resorted to issuing Circulating Bearer Cash Cheques for as much as 60 million Yuan.

It should be said that the Chinese people were quite used to inflation. The war-lords who had issued notes at will had never concerned themselves with matters of redemption. One such war-lord, General Feng, started the Bank of the Northwest without any capital at all. Asked what backed his currency issues he disarmingly replied: 'The bayonets of my soldiers'. General Feng, incidentally, turned Christian and required his army to share his new enlightenment. He achieved this by having the entire army corps march past him while he baptized them with his garden hose.

Japan

When the Japanese founded Manchukuo, all the paper money in Kirin had to be changed over. The Japanese were slightly surprised to find that Kirin had saddled the market with 10.3 billion of Tiao in paper money. The militarists, unable to offer any security, had inscribed the notes with pious quotes from the classics. So one reads: 'The Wei River flows eastward. When it reaches Yangchow I shall drop two tears into it and request you, oh River, to bring them to my home'. The Japanese were not impressed and gave an exchange ratio of 500 to 1 for the new Manchukuo yuan – which, as usual, made the poor even poorer.

The Japanese, however, were to experience inflation themselves. Japan had prepared well for its sudden and massive invasion of the Pacific areas in World War II and banknotes were printed carefully in advance of the event. Her declared intention was to create a Greater East Asia Co-Prosperity Sphere, which would effectively create an empire for Japan.

Collectors refer to these notes as 'JIM', standing for Japanese Invasion Money. There were five major areas of issue which have, in most cases, a similarity of design, namely Burma, Malaya, Netherlands East Indies, Oceania and the Philippines. They can be identified easily because the prefix letter is the first letter of the country name. So B stands for Burma, M for Malaya, O for Oceania, S for Netherlands East Indies (Sumatra) and P for Philippines.

Malaya (**13**) was one of the first territories to succumb to the Japanese, who landed at Kota Bharu in northen Malaya on 8 December 1941, and just over two months later received the surrender of General Percival in Singapore. Early note issues had serial numbers as well as prefix letters and were engraved. As inflation took hold, the Japanese decided to do away with serial numbers altogether. For speed and cheapness, later issues were lithographed instead of engraved.

Burma is another territory with a maze of Japanese invasion notes. The Japanese were not considered hostile by many of the native population and the Burmese prime minister, U. Saw, supported them. He was arrested by the British on 18 January 1942, but on that same day General Shojiro Lida moved the 15th Army from northern Thailand into Burma. Mandalay fell on 21

13 1,000 dollar note of the Japanese Occupation of Malaya in World War II. By the end of the war Japanese pay-officers no longer bothered to count the notes – they used a measuring stick.

May in the same year, and the British, having retreated to India, began the long bitter struggle which took Allied troops through 1,000 miles of the world's worst jungles, to win back the territory. Many British soldiers can remember kicking Japanese invasion money about like confetti in the streets when they re-entered Mandalay.

In the Philippines some senior Japanese officers took the view that General MacArthur would honour the Japanese occupation issues rather than see the Philippine people suffer, so they began printing some high denomination notes for 1,000 pesos, hoping to benefit from them. Indeed it is now known that some notes were printed in Baguio after United States troops had captured Manila. As many Philippine residents had literally sacks full of notes by this time, the Japanese War Notes Claimants Association Inc., was formed with a view to getting the notes redeemed. The association used three distinct types of over-stamps. Early overprints read: 'Japanese War Notes Claimants/Received for/ . . . (signature) SAFEKEEPING /Association of the Philippines Inc'. Later overprints were abbreviated to 'Compiled/ JAPWANCAP Inc.' and another reads: 'Japanese War Notes Claimants Association of the Philippines'. But the Americans were not interested in redeeming the Japanese issues and they are still about in large quantities.

14 Bolivia was one of the South American nations to suffer a major inflation in 1985. Denominations such as this 5000 pesos were once 'high' denominations, but now have virtually no face value.

Current inflation issues

Collectors will find plenty of inflation issues to be had among the current issues of the world. Quite recently inflation became so bad in Israel that the authorities decided that the 1 shekel note was useless; it cost more in time and effort to count and handle the notes than the face value was worth – so they burned them. These notes will probably be regarded as quite scarce among collectors because of this.

In 1981 Argentina became the only country in the world with a circulating note for a million denomination. Inflation swept its value away and it was replaced with a new unit, the peso argentino. One million pesos were worth 100 pesos argentinos. By 1985 inflation was at 1010 per cent and Argentina has begun phasing out the peso altogether. The new unit, the austral (South), was valued at $1.25. The first issue of the new australs were in the form of overprints on the 10,000 pesos argentinos.

It was not long before other South American nations were following Argentina with million denominations. Bolivia (**14**) has been issuing 'cheque gerencias' for denominations up to a million bolivianos. Bolivia's new president, Victor Paz Estenssoro, took over his position with inflation running at 8,900 per cent and with officials predicting that it could top 50,000 per cent the next year. Brazil and Mexico were showing signs of inflation getting out of hand in 1985.

15 The last note of Cambodia, for 1,000 riels. It was never issued because the Pol Pot instituted an 'agrarian moneyless society' in the newly named nation, Kampuchea.

Although many collectors will have suffered in the sense that when they obtained a note it had a much higher value than now, it is nevertheless worth studying them carefully. Quite a few will be found with 'early' signature combinations, which may well turn out to be quite scarce in the long run.

A good example of this is Cambodia, now called Kampuchea (**15**). The floods of notes which have come on the market were not, however, the result of inflation as such. The Khmer Rouge (communist insurgents) under Pol Pot suddenly announced that there would be no more money. Kampuchea would be an agrarian moneyless society. At the same time they evicted everyone from the capital city and set them to work in the fields. Refugees brought stacks of notes into Thailand, from where they have come onto the collectors' market, but it is only the later signature combinations that came out in huge quantities. All these notes are worth a second look. The 100 riels, 1970 issue, showing ceremonial oxen, is catalogued at $1.25 because of the total devaluation, but the same note with earlier signatures is catalogued at $50.

7
Notes of the United Kingdom

Modern notes of the Bank of England

One of the pleasures of collecting modern Bank of England notes is that the collector can either opt for one of each type of note, or can attempt to get a complete collection of all the serial letters found on the notes. The term 'modern' Bank of England notes is applied to those issued from November 1928. It is a convenient starting date because in that month the Bank of England took over total responsibility for the issue and redemption of notes. During World War I, the Treasury had issued the £1 and 10s. notes. Also there is no possibility of anyone forming a complete collection of the earlier notes – most of them have never been seen by twentieth-century collectors. But the 1928 issues onwards present an opportunity to get a complete collection for those prepared to stick at it and search out the difficult prefix letters, for the £1 and 10s. notes. The higher denominations tend to be difficult to find and expensive; so most collectors elect for a representative collection of them while attempting a complete collection of the £1 and 10s.

The prefixes used on these notes become of great importance in determining value. The first of the modern Chief Cashiers was Cyril Patrick Mahon, whose signature is found on the 1928 issue. A complete collection of the 10s. notes of Mahon consists of six notes: prefixes A, Z, Y, X, W and V. That is the order in which they were issued and shows immediately that the Bank of England did not issue in alphabetical order. The Type collector will settle for one of the commoner prefixes which catalogue at £30 in Very Fine condition. But the A01 prefix catalogues at £250 in Extremely Fine condition and is very hard to get. Only one million of this inaugural run were issued. The last prefix is V and this too is rare because only 11 million are known to have been issued, that is, V01 to V11. Purist collectors will pay a premium for first and last prefixes so the desirable notes are V01 and V11. Although these are modern notes, the fact is that we do not know which letter was used for a Replacement note, and while the note is given a catalogue number it simply says 'not yet traced'.

Replacement notes are known for most issues. They were used to replace damaged or badly printed notes which were being taken out and destroyed. Naturally they tend to be scarce because not many were needed.

Unique to Mahon issues are the presentation notes. To mark the issue the Bank of England prepared £1 and 10s. notes with matching serial numbers in presentation parchment envelopes inscribed 'Bank of England, 22 November 1928'. Only a hundred such pairs are believed to have been issued. Recently a pair in a perfectly preserved envelope was sold for £2000.

Basil Gage Catterns became Chief Cashier in 1929 and the 10s. note bearing his signature can be found with ten different prefix letters. The first of these is V and the earliest known number is 14. Obviously the numbering took over from the previous cashier's last 10s. note which was traced to V11. What happened to V12 and V13 is not yet known. Perhaps they circulated but have just not been preserved or one may turn up. If it does it will command a premium. This is the sort of thing that experienced collectors are on the look out for.

Catterns £1 notes are found with fifteen prefix letters starting with H, traced from H33, again a change-over from Mahon where the last £1 note was H32. The last letter for this series is Z. First and last prefixes catalogue at £40 and £35 respectively while the middle range of letters are only £25. The first Replacement note which can be positively identified is in this series. It is the letter A and catalogues at £75.

Purist collectors recognise the use of two different plates for the printing of Mahon and Catterns notes and some of the succeeding issues. Plate 1 is identified by the signature block width, which for Catterns 10s. is 126mm while Plate 2 is 128mm. For the £1 note, Plate 1 is 137.5mm and Plate 2 138.5m.

The next cashier was Kenneth Oswald Peppiatt, who was Chief Cashier throughout World War II, and whose signature is found on notes from 1934 to 1949. There are so many different notes of this period that collectors divide them into recognised periods. The first period is from 1934 to the outbreak of war in 1939. The first series of 10s. notes have seven different prefix letters issued in the order, J,H,E,D,C,B,A. So here, A is the last prefix letter. Up to now, with the solitary exception of the Catterns £1 Replacement note __A, which has the numbers 01A to 99A, all the prefixes preceded the numbers. Now there is a change. The second series of Peppiatt 10s. notes are Z,Y,X,W,U,T,S,R and O, but with the numbers preceding the prefix letter, eg. O1Z, with Z and O being the first and last of the series. The £1 notes also have the number before the letter for the first series but the second series changes to two letters for each note, i.e. A03A, B01A and so on.

Collectors distinguish the next issue of Peppiatt notes by calling them 'Second Period'. The colour is changed from the familiar green to blue on the £1 note, and from red-brown to mauve on the 10s. note. A metal thread, the invention of Mr S.B. Chamberlain, General Manager of the Bank's Printing Works, was introduced as a war-time security measure. But War bombing interfered with banknote production at this time and the first blue notes were produced at St Luke's Printing Works, London. They are known as the 'A series' because the three prefix combinations are A__D, A__E and A__H. Then after the printing works had been bombed, printing was transferred to Overton in Hampshire where a much larger issue was made using other letters of the alphabet. The collector needs no less than fifty-five letter combinations to get a complete set, with a possibility of yet another two, Y__H and Z__H which have not been traced so far, but theoretically exist.

At this time there was a great fear that the German forces would invade England and the Government were concerned that coins would be hoarded and difficulties arise in transporting coinage. The Bank of England was instructed to prepare fractional notes for use if the invasion came. These were 5s. and 2s.6d. notes which were hurriedly printed and distributed to the main clearing houses ready for issue. When the invasion scare had passed orders were given for them to be destroyed. A few have survived.

Third Period £1 notes were issued in 1948 and these were really a reissue of the unthreaded pre-war notes. They are quite scarce by comparison with other issues, and are easily identified by the prefixes R__A and S__A, the latter being the more expensive as it is only traced to S48A.

16 Standard design of Bank of England £1 notes at the start of the 'modern' period in 1928. Apart from changes of signature and one colour change, to blue during an emergency period, they were in use in this form until 1960. This note was issued in 1948 by Chief Cashier K.O. Peppiatt.

Fourth period Peppiatt notes re-introduce the metal thread, and the prefix S_ _A, which starts the series, overlaps the previous issue of S_ _A. Overlapping prefixes are, of course, more valuable, especially when they can be tied down to a number. But in this case they cannot because the previous issue has been traced to S48A and the new issue starts at S39A. Exactly why the numbers were not issued consecutively is a puzzle for research students. There are thirteen prefix combinations, the last being H_ _B (**16**), which is thought by many to be as difficult to find as the first prefix, as it has only been traced to H39B.

The Replacement £1 notes of this series are identified by the letters S_ _S and are very scarce. They are only known printed from So1S to So9S and catalogue at £125 in EF condition. One mistake that many new collectors have made is to hand over their money quickly when they see a green pound with the prefix S_ _S at a much lower price – only to find that it is a much later replacement note issued by Beale. The valuable replacement is the Peppiatt signature. The fourth period of Peppiatt notes also includes a rare 10s. with the prefix _ _L, only known from 72L (catalogued at £125) – and a rare replacement 10s. note prefixed 01A to 03A which catalogues at £145.

The next cashier was Percival Spencer Beale (1949–55) and many of these notes are commonly found. Taking the 10s. issues, there were two types of prefix lettering plus the replacement. The first starts with number, number, E and is catalogued at £125 because the series only started at 92E. Then comes _ _D, _ _D, which are £16, and then B, the last series. The second issue of 10s. notes have two prefix letters and start Z01Z followed by fifteen middle combinations of letters and then the last prefix D_ _Z, a scarcer than normal issue as it is only known to D85Z. The replacement notes are prefixed between 05A and 35A with a catalogue value of £75. The £1 notes have three different series of letters, the first starting H_ _B and going J_ _B, K_ _B, L_ _B, etc. The next series starts A_ _C, B_ _C, C_ _C and so on and the final series A_ _J, B_ _J, C_ _J, etc. The replacement £1 note is S10S to S70S, following on from the Peppiatt replacement notes which ended at S09S.

In 1955, Leslie Kenneth O'Brien became Chief Cashier and the note issues became more extensive. The replacement £1 notes carry on from the previous cashier, now prefixed S71S to S99S and as that completed the number sequence new letters were introduced from S01T, but these only went to S22T and are therefore scarcer than the O'Brien replacements. All issues of 10s. and £1 notes have double letter prefixes and the only really scarce ones are the first prefix 10s. which is D86Z, and the last prefix £1, which is traced only from K01L to K13L.

During O'Brien's term as Chief Cashier the note design was changed and the notes show a portrait of Queen Elizabeth II (**17**). This was the first time in the long history of the Bank of England that a reigning monarch was featured on the notes. They first appeared in 1960. The £1 and 10s. notes were designed by Robert Austin and were first printed by the intaglio process in sheets of twenty-four at the Bank of England Works, Loughton, Essex. For some reason the Bank of England decided to change the prefix letters of replacement notes which for these issues are identified by the letter M.

At this time there was a lot of experimenting with the printing of notes. There was a need for more notes and so a need for quicker production. Instead of bringing in sheets of twenty-four, a new method was experimented with, using a reel-fed web press developed in conjunction with the Bank's engineers and Masson, Scott, Thrissell Engineering Ltd. These notes were put into circulation without any publicity and the general public noticed

17 In 1960, for the first time ever, the portrait of a reigning monarch, Queen Elizabeth II, appeared on Bank of England £1 notes. The general design with minor modifications lasted until 1978. This note has a replacement prefix, MS.

nothing amiss. It was only after their circulation that collectors became aware of them, which accounts for their great rarity. The notes can be identified by the following prefixes: A01N, A05N and A06N. On the reverse, just above the bottom panel 'Bank of England' is a small letter 'R', which stands for 'Research'. Such notes catalogue at £145. They were printed in 1961.

The following year a new Chief Cashier took office, Jasper Quintus Hollom, and the further development of the reel-fed machine led to the introduction of a web press by Goebel Darmstad. The notes printed from this machine can be identified by the small letter 'G' for 'Goebel' in the same place as the previous letter 'R'. This proved successful and all notes were then printed by reel-fed machines (four in all) supplied by Masson, Scott, Thrissell Ltd. It is interesting to note that the reels of paper are two miles long, and can print something like two million notes in a day.

Collectors will find it comparatively easy to complete a prefix collection of £1 and 10s. notes of the next cashier, John Standish Fforde (1966–70). The first £1 prefix, B__Y catalogues at £28 and there is one scarce replacement issue, T__M. The T__M replacement prefix has been traced without the 'G' reverse from T01M to T04M and with the 'G' reverse from T29M to T32M. A lot of replacement notes seem to have been printed, for prefixes are known for M__R, M__N, R__M, S__M, U__M, T__M and N__M.

18 The last design of the Bank of England £1 note, introduced in 1978. The £1 note has now been withdrawn from circulation and the very last prefix combination used was DY21.

One event of some importance was that the 10*s*. note went out of production altogether. The last printing was in 1967 with prefixes A__N, B__N, C__N and D__N and the last series was traced to D38N.

From 1970 to 1980 John Brangwyn Page was Chief Cashier, and again this is an easy series to complete except perhaps for the very first £1 prefix which is only known with three numbers, S87L, S89L and S90L and has a catalogue value of £25. Because of the printing methods it is possible to get notes with consecutive numbers but with different Chief Cashiers, i.e. J.S. Fforde and J.B. Page, which are highly prized among collectors and fetch over £60 a pair. In fact for two years £1 notes were issued with signatures of Page and Fforde concurrently which caused many prefixes to be shared by both cashiers.

A new design for the £1 note was introduced in 1978, smaller in size, with Sir Isaac Newton on the reverse. The new notes had only one serial number instead of the normal two. The last £1 notes were printed with the signature of David Henry Fitzroy Somerset, who became Chief Cashier in 1980. Prefix letters are now two together, e.g. AN01, BN01. The very last run of £1 notes, which fetch over £20 each, is DY21 (**18**).

The higher denomination notes present quite a variety. Up to 1957 the old familiar white notes had served for all high denominations. They had been used, with very little alteration in design, since the founding of the Bank of England in 1694. The last printing of the white £5 was dated 20 September 1956 and the last prefix was D99A. A new, multi-coloured £5 note designed by Stephen Gooden was issued in 1957. This features a vignette of Britannia helmeted. In fact the whole series of notes had been designed with the Britannia helmeted, but only the £5 was actually issued. Specimens exist with the signature P.S. Beale, for 10s. and £1 notes as well. The new £5 can be found in two varieties; on one, the £5 signs on the reverse are in outline only, and in the other variety they are shaded in dark blue.

In 1963 the £5 note was changed, using a design by Reynolds Stone, featuring the Queen's portrait on the obverse and Britannia seated with shield on the reverse, for which the artist's daughter was used as a model. In 1964 a £10 note was introduced, with the same Queen's portrait, but a reverse of a lion holding a key, and in 1970 a £20 note made its appearance, designed by Harry Eccleston, with a statue of Shakespeare from the Kent Memorial in Westminster Abbey on the reverse.

The design for the £10 note was changed in 1975 with a Florence Nightingale reverse, and in 1971 the £5 was also changed with a Duke of Wellington reverse. Both these notes were smaller than the previous issues. The £5 can be found with a little letter 'L' on the reverse to the right of the £5 denomination, which stands for 'Lithograph'. In 1980, under Chief Cashier Somerset, some experimental notes were produced for the £5 for Optical Character Recognition. They appear to be extremely rare but can be recognised at once by the number 91. Serial letters traced are AN91, BR91, CS91, DT91, EU91, HW91, JX91, KY91 and LZ91.

A £50 note was introduced in 1981 showing Sir Christopher Wren on the reverse. For security the £20 note was slightly modified recently and appeared with the straight metal thread changed to an interrupted line thread.

Early notes of the Bank of England

Collecting the early notes of the Bank of England is a difficult and very expensive task. It should be remembered that all issues of the Bank of England are still honoured to the extent of their face value. The first notes of 1694 are known as Running Cash Notes and were written out by hand on ordinary paper bought from a stationer. In this the Bank of England was merely copying the goldsmith notes which had become so prominent during the reign of Charles I and were deposit receipts for gold or silver made out to the bearer who could then use the note in a business transaction rather than withdraw the deposited gold for the transaction.

Very little is known about another type of issue, known as Sealed Bills. They were not actual banknotes in a strict sense but were interest bearing promissory notes. They do not appear to have been popular and went out of use within twenty years.

Then there were Acceptable Notes which came into use only four days after the Running Cash notes. They were certificates of deposit and gave the depositer the right to 'draw' notes on the Bank of England. Any such withdrawals were noted on the Acceptable note by endorsement. A 'check' pattern form was introduced for the depositor to draw his note on, which, of course, was effectively a type of cheque.

These notes were superseded in about 1699 by the part-printed note. These had a printed medallion of Britannia but the amounts were written in by hand. None of these notes is known to exist in private hands and it is not until 1778–1807 when Abraham Newland was Chief Cashier that collectors can really hope to obtain material. At this time white £1 and £2 notes were introduced (1797) and exist in various forms. Some of the £2 notes are found with the denomination block at an angle (**19**). This was done so that illiterate people could identify them from the ordinary £1 note. Newland was a workaholic and became famous for never sleeping away from the Bank. He declined a pension, having saved a fortune, for those days, amounting to £200,000 and was given a special presentation of silver-plate valued at 1000 guineas instead.

When Newland died the next Chief Cashier should have been Robert Aslett, the second cashier. But he was found guilty of embezzling and had lodged Exchequer Bills as security for advances with a lottery office in Cornhill. He was lucky to escape the death penalty but was imprisoned until 1820 and pardoned on condition he left the country.

In his place came the 'reluctant' Chief Cashier, Henry Hase, who regretted the circumstances that led to his promotion. During his term branch notes were introduced which bore the name of the town they were issued in 'here or in London'. Notes became fully printed except for signatures at this time and

19 Bank of England £1 and £2 notes issued in the early 1800s. Notice the 'Two' is at an angle, to help illiterates to distinguish it from the £1 note.

branch notes were issued at Gloucester, Manchester, Swansea, Birmingham, Liverpool, Bristol, Leeds, Exeter, Newcastle, and later at Hull and Plymouth. Some of the branch notes are extremely rare even though they may have twentieth-century dates. The scarcest of all are Plymouth, Bristol and Exeter.

Following Henry Hase came Thomas Rippon, Matthew Marshall, William Miller, George Forbes (**20**), Frank May, Horace George Bowen, all of whose notes are extremely rare although in recent years a few Bowen notes (**21**) have come on to the market, fetching an average of £500 each.

With the change of Chief Cashier to John Gordon Nairne (1902–18) the collector comes to items which are available on the

20 Bank of England £5 issued in 1869 under Chief Cashier George Forbes, but signed by one of his staff, H. Dixon. Such items are extreme rarities and not priced in catalogues.

21 Bank of England £5 issued by Chief Cashier H.G. Bowen (1893–1902). Priced at £1,250 in catalogues, a small hoard came out in the 1980s and the market price dropped to around £500.

---

market and the only question here is how much to pay for them. Seldom are they offered at less than £200 in VF condition and mostly turn up in VG condition. When Ernest Harvey became Chief Cashier in 1918 the notes become more easily available to collectors and can be obtained for as little as £40. But new collectors should realise that all these notes are rarities and to form a collection of the early white notes is not even a matter of wealth, but a matter of availability. The £5 denomination is the common one; higher denominations have no set value, as they so seldom come up for sale at all.

22 Bank of England £1,000 of 1938 – the highest denomination ever issued to the public by the Bank.

The Bank of England in its time has issued white note denominations of £1, £2, £5, £10, £15, £20, £30, £40, £50, £100, £200, £300, £500 and £1,000 (**22**). All the high denominations above £5 were discontinued after 1943 and all branch notes ceased to be issued at the outbreak of war in 1939. At this time Kenneth Oswald Peppiatt (1934–49) was Chief Cashier. The only known white £1 notes are dated between 1797 and 1826, when they disappeared from circulation as the public preferred gold sovereigns.

Treasury notes

The Bank of England was not the only issuer of notes on a national scale. Treasury notes were introduced at the outbreak of World War I. These are quite fascinating and came about through nothing more than 'school-boy' jealousy of the old public school system. For centuries the Bank of England had adequately maintained the note production of England but some of the Treasury officials were keen to have their own notes. The opportunity came with the outbreak of war. There was no such thing as a pound note or a ten shilling note in circulation as sovereigns were the currency for anything under £5.

23 Third issue £1 Treasury note signed by John Bradbury. The reverse shows the Houses of Parliament. Note the serial number.

It was recognised that war would cause a hoarding of gold coin and that there would soon be a problem, so the Bank of England had prepared designs for a £1 note in advance. It was a white £1, smaller than the £5, but otherwise quite similar. It is hard to understand why the rough designs of the first Treasury notes should be preferred to the well executed white £1. It appears that no official choice was made and that the Treasury notes came into circulation through Treasury guile and Lloyd George in particular, who was most careful not to reveal his hand until the matter was a *fait accompli*.

The Treasury had one major problem; banknote paper. They could hardly go to the Bank of England and ask for paper. They solved the problem by using supplies of postage stamp paper, bearing the watermark known to philatelists as the Multiple Royal Cypher 'Simple'. The notes were small, hurriedly and very badly designed and were signed by the Secretary to the Treasury, Sir John Bradbury. On 7 August 1914 the £1 (black on white) was issued, and a week later the 10s. (red on white). The Currency and Bank Notes Act was rushed through Parliament on 5 August giving the notes legal tender status and the August Bank holiday was extended for three clear days while the notes were printed in round the clock shifts.

24 Attractive green coloured ten shilling note of the Treasury signed by Warren Fisher.

But the designs were so terrible that almost immediately the Treasury decided on new designs, which were issued three months later. Even the Chairman of the Board of Inland Revenue had commented that he preferred the design of the school leaving certificate! The new notes were larger, more like our normal size, remained black on white and red on white, but were now at least reasonably designed and well printed. But they were not considered totally satisfactory and it was left to Bertram Mackennal, designer of the coinage, to come up with the third Treasury note designs (**23**). These showed St George and the Dragon on the obverse, together with the King's portrait, and the Houses of Parliament on the reverse. All the notes signed by John Bradbury were quickly nicknamed 'Bradburys'. Later issues were signed by the next Treasury official, Warren Fisher (**24**) and the last issue of Treasury notes recognised the partition of Ireland, a little belatedly in 1927, by changing the title to include 'Northern Ireland'.

One issue of particular interest to collectors is the Arabic-overprinted £1 and 10s. (**25**). This was the only occasion on which British notes were printed with a foreign language on them. The history and exact reason for issue is still disputed. The Treasury minute indicates that they were issued for the British

25 The famous 'Dardanelles' overprint in Arabic on the Treasury ten shilling note. Both £1 and 10s. were overprinted during World War I – the only time British notes were overprinted in a foreign language.

Military Expeditionary Forces in the Mediterranean and the Naval Expeditionary Forces. But they are generally referred to as Dardanelles Campaign notes; and there is evidence that they were quickly withdrawn after the failure of the campaign. Letters I have seen from serving personnel are contradictory, but the notes are mentioned as being issued as pay to soldiers in Gallipoli. At all events, they are extremely rare, and the £1 usually fetches around £2,000 in Uncirculated condition.

Naturally during all this period relations between the Treasury officials and the Bank of England were a little sour and it was not until 28 November 1928 that the Bank of England was finally able to resume total responsibility for the issue of banknotes for the nation. They took over redemption responsibilities for the Treasury notes, which like all Bank of England notes are still valid to the extent of their face value on presentation to the Bank of England.

The Treasury notes had, however, prevented public fear which would certainly have grown if the facts had been available. When German troops moved to assist the Austrians, the effect on finance had been immediate. Banks called in their money from the bill-brokers and this caused a drain on the Bank of England. The Bank Rate went up to eight per cent, the London Stock

Exchange closed and the mid-August Settling Day had to be postponed. The Bank Charter Act of 1844 (obliging the Bank to pay out in gold) was suspended. When, on 4 August 1914, England declared war, the Bank had only £9 million gold reserve. The Fiduciary issue was £18,450,000, but against all this England did have favourable trade balances of £207 million and a further £4,000 million in foreign securities.

Provincial Banks

Over 900 different banks operating from the provinces have issued banknotes in the UK at various times. These notes are known as provincial banknotes to differentiate them from the Bank of England and Treasury issues. Most of these banks failed, and the notes became irredeemable, but quite a few amalgamated into the major banking organisations that we have today, like Barclays, Westminster and Lloyds, and those notes would still be redeemed if presented today. The early banks were all private banks, operated by partnerships under common law and the partners were liable for any debts. But in 1826, joint stock banks came into being, allowing more than six partners, but restricting their business to within sixty-five miles of London to prevent any serious threat to the Bank of England.

The 'Bible' for collectors of this series is *The Standard Catalogue of Provincial Banks and Banknotes* by Geoffrey L. Grant, published by Spinks. The first of its kind, this mammoth work sets out to list all the known provincial banks and their issues. There is a great deal of research to be done and our knowledge of these issues is very incomplete. They have the added interest of relating to local history and are often hand-signed by the men who developed the major towns and cities in the country.

Most dealers have a small stock of these provincial notes and they still tend to be underpriced in relation to their true rarity. This is because so many different banks existed at one time or another that there are always some notes about. But a note found in a dealers' stock for £22 may in practice be one of only ten or twenty known. There are a few banks where the notes are very common, usually because large hoards of the cancelled notes (often cancelled by having the signature cut out) were held in the bank instead of being destroyed and have subsequently come on to the market.

It is an area of collecting where condition has to be judged in relation to availability. To try and form a collection in Extremely Fine condition would be almost impossible today and would certainly be very limited in its scope. Most collectors will settle for notes in Very Fine condition and for the rare notes would be happy to take them VG. Often such notes are found literally cut in half and stuck together again. There was a very good reason for this. To avoid the risk of letting them fall into the hands of highwaymen, banks would often send a consignment of one half of each note by coach, and the other halves by another coach at a later time. An employee would then match them up at their destination and stick them together again. In some cases specially prepared and printed labels were used for joining the notes together, bearing a bank imprint.

From 1750 private banks flourished in Great Britain and, with few restrictions imposed on them at that time, denominations appeared for the most unlikely sums, including pence. The majority of the population could not read or write, and this led to the early 'skit' notes, which later developed into advertising or propaganda issues. They were often accepted as currency by illiterate people. One, issued in Scotland for a penny, even contained an option clause and read: 'Promise to pay to Thomas Tailor or the bearer on demand, one penny, sterling, or in option of the directors Three Ballads, six days after demand . . .' Many of the skit notes related to the Napoleonic wars.

Sooner or later the collector comes across the Fort Montague Bank with its issue for five halfpence, showing a picture of a fort with the Union Jack flying proudly over it. Even stranger are the notes with denominations in hours. They are known as the Robert Owen Labour notes. Owen, publisher of *Crisis in 1832*, and an early socialist, developed ideas of co-operation among the workers. He opened the London Exchange Bazaar between 1832 and 1834, and used a system of finance based on hours worked. Pricing was done by special valuers who worked out the raw materials used and the labour time taken in producing the item. The producer was then given paper money to that value in 'labour hours'. The idealistic scheme had little chance of succeeding and eventually Owen had to close it down. But it is to his credit that he made good the deficit, amounting to some £2,000, out of his own pocket.

Just about every private and joint-stock bank has an interesting history behind it. As an example let us take just one bank, Jonathan Backhouse and Co. Notes from this bank are still easily available in cancelled form. The bank was established at Darlington in 1798 (it had started in 1774 as Backhouse and Co.), and was later to amalgamate with Barclays in 1896. Jonathan Backhouse & Co. was prominent in the early history of Barclays Bank, and one of its directors was on the board of Barclays.

Lord Darlington did not like Backhouse and attempted to 'break the bank', by instructing his tenants to pay their rents in Backhouse notes, intending to amass the notes and then suddenly present them to Backhouse, anticipating that he would not be able to honour them. Jonathan Backhouse was warned of the inpending attempt and rushed to London to obtain bullion in order to meet the notes. On his return journey his coach was passing through Croft when a front wheel came off the vehicle. Cruikshank has left us a charming picture of the event, entitled: 'Balancing the cash'. For Jonathan Backhouse had no time to wait for repairs, he balanced the cash on one side of the coach and drove on furiously with just three wheels. He arrived in time, paid out in gold the large quantity of notes presented by Lord Darlington's agent, and then said to him: 'Now tell thy master that if he will sell Raby (his home) I will pay for it with the same metal.'

Maberly Phillips, author of *A History of Banks, Bankers and Banking*, records another incident involving Backhouse, who, dressed in the plain attire of the Society of Friends, was in a tavern when made the subject of ridicule by a traveller. On being challenged to a bet, Backhouse responded that he did not bet, but to show his indifference to money would burn £5 notes, note for note, with the traveller. Phillips wrote: 'Mr Backhouse offered to repeat the process, but the commercial, considerably cowed, declined. Mr Backhouse quietly thanked him for burning one of his (Backhouse) notes, for which he had received £5, while the note he, Mr Backhouse, had burned, was of his own bank, and had only cost him the paper.'

In most collecting fields the general rule is that the older the item is, the more scarce it is likely to be. The opposite is true in the case of private banknotes. There were several severe depressions in England in the eighteenth century, and in one, in 1772, five

26 £5 of the Chesterfield and North Derbyshire Bank. Started in 1834 it failed and was taken over in 1878, by Crompton and Evans which itself was taken over by Parr's Bank Ltd in 1894.

---

hundred and twenty-five banks went bankrupt, leaving numbers of irredeemable paper notes.

The Bank Act of 1844 set about regulating the note-issues and on that date of the Act, 6 May, only those banks currently issuing notes could continue to do so, and the maximum amount they were allowed to circulate was rigidly restricted. When banks merged, the circulation of the absorbed bank would be lost. Gradually the number of banks issuing notes was reduced (**26**, **27**). By the 1890s there were only around twenty banks still able to issue notes under strict control and it follows that these are now much scarcer than the earlier notes issued without restriction. The last provincial bank to issue notes in England was Fox, Fowler of Wellington, whose final issue was made in 1921, before that firm joined Lloyds Bank.

One of the main sources of information for collectors of provincial notes are the quite considerable number of books published by the banks themselves. Most of the major banks, like Barclays, National Westminster and Lloyds have well-documented histories, and so do many of the long-standing banks, like Coutts. Collectors will find public libraries very useful in tracing specific histories. Very often there are pictures of long-forgotten note issues and details of issue.

27 One of the last private banks to issue notes, Beckett and Co., Leeds Bank. This £5 is dated 1920; in 1921 the bank joined the London County Westminster.

Scotland

More than any other part of the United Kingdom, Scotland has issued a wide variety of colourful notes in its long banking history. Counting changes in title, nearly a hundred different banks have issued notes in Scotland. Unlike their British counterparts which often went bankrupt and saw note-holders suffering, Scottish banks always honoured the notes in the hands of the general public – on occasions other Scottish banks honoured them in the full knowledge that the bank had collapsed. As a result of this only directors and shareholders have ever suffered when a Scottish bank failed – which did not happen very often – and there has always been great confidence in Scotland in the circulating paper money.

In Scotland banknotes were not just more convenient than gold, they were as good as gold. This explains why so few of the older issues of Scotland have survived. Collectors of these notes are fortunate for the series has been tabulated and studied, probably better than any other area of paper money, by the late James Douglas, banker, archivist and author, who assembled one of the finest collections of Scottish notes ever known. In 1975 he wrote the standard work on Scottish notes, *Scottish Banknotes* published by Stanley Gibbons Publications Ltd., with detailed descriptions and histories of over eight-hundred 'face different' notes, from eighty banks.

28 £1 note (12 pounds Scots) of the Bank of Scotland, dated 1723. Although the Bank of Scotland issued £1 notes as early as 1704, the only known earlier date than the 1723 issue is an example in the archive dated 1716 and with Edinburgh spelt 'Edenburgh'.

Mr Douglas then began to compile specialist volumes, and the first of these, *20th Century Scottish Banknotes*, dealing with the Bank of Scotland, British Linen Bank and Union Bank, was published in 1984 by Banking Memorabilia, shortly before the author's death. This work lists every single prefix and the exact number of notes printed in each case. His volume on the Royal Bank of Scotland, completed by Dr R.W. Pringle, was published in 1986.

Early Scottish banking started with the Bank of Scotland

issuing notes for £5, £10, £20, £50, and £100, just one year after the Bank of England had issued notes. It was not until 1704 that a £1 note (**28**) was produced in Scotland; at that time the denomination was £12 Scots, the equivalent of £1 sterling. The monopoly enjoyed by the Bank of Scotland lapsed and in 1727 a new bank, The Royal Bank of Scotland, opened its doors and immediately issued notes.

The two giants were soon at each other's throats as they engaged in fierce competition. At times there was a shortage of coin and one bank would collect a large amount of the other's notes and then suddenly present them for redemption, hoping the bank could not meet its obligations. Just how close the Bank of Scotland came to fall foul of this manoeuvre is shown by the fact that in 1730 they introduced the 'Option Clause' on notes. The notes were then payable on demand or at the option of the directors six months after presentation with addition of interest at the current rate. This effectively put a stop to the Royal Bank's efforts to embarrass the Bank of Scotland.

The Bank of Scotland did not forget, and many years later applied the same technique which resulted in 1761 with the Royal Bank also implementing the Option Clause. All these notes are extremely rare today. One of the major early banks of Scotland was The British Linen Bank Company. Established in 1746, its main function was merchandising linen; it introduced promissory notes to assist its main enterprise and in fact not until 1849 was the company recognised as a banking corporation. In 1763 the company stopped trading in linen altogether and concentrated on the more lucrative business of banking. Collectors will find that many of the Scottish banks have interesting histories behind them (**29, 30, 31**).

One peculiarity of Scottish banking affects condition. The large £20 notes (20.6 × 13cm) were folded over twice for delivery to the banks. In consequence all these notes should have two light folds on them and are still truly 'uncirculated'. Those which have no folds have been pressed for the collector market!

Another oddity about Scottish notes is that the £10 note went out of fashion. No-one can quite explain why, but suddenly four of the eight major banks of issue stopped producing the note in the first half of the twentieth century, and the other four only had small isolated printings of the £10 note. By the 1930s only the

29 The portrait of King William IV appears on £20 notes of the Western Bank of Scotland in 1832. Illustrations of the Royal Exchange and Glasgow Cathedral flank the portrait.

30 Proof of £10 note of Central Bank of Scotland for the 1866 issue. A joint stock bank established at Perth in 1834, it was purchased by the Bank of Scotland in 1868. At that time there were 405 shareholders and notes in circulation had a value of only £42,933. Beautifully engraved by W.H Lizars, such notes are extremely rare.

31 North of Scotland Bank £100 of 1930, featuring the Marischal College, Aberdeen.

Bank of Scotland was issuing a £10 note and in fact printed only 50,000 over a period of thirty-four years. Then, in 1963, a special printing was made of 50,000 on 26 September 1963, and again on the next day, 27 September. The note still proved unpopular and the majority of these notes remained in cold storage at the head office, and were later incinerated. They are now very scarce. When in 1970 the Bank of Scotland introduced the Walter Scott series of notes, they in fact omitted the £10 and only added it later in 1974. So £10 notes are worth looking for in the Scottish series.

Ireland

Irish banknotes are as fascinating as any other issues of the United Kingdom and with the creation of the Irish Free State brought about a position where some banks, like the Provincial Bank of Ireland Ltd. were issuing in two separate countries. The earliest private notes date to the end of the eighteenth century and are very hard to obtain.

It is necessary to understand something of the history of Ireland to follow the banknote issues. The Easter Rising of 1916 led to a struggle for independence and in December 1918 Sinn Fein, the separatist party, won seventy-three seats in the General

32 The famous Lady Lavery portrait found on many notes of the Irish Free State Currency Commision and Central Bank issues. It was engraved by John Harrison and was used from 1928 to 1977. The 10*s*. and £1 notes have a face portrait only.

Election, the Unionists won twenty-six and the old Irish Parliamentary Party only had 6. Sinn Fein refused to take their seats in Westminster and met in Dublin as the Dail Eireann, declaring independence. They were declared illegal and the shooting began. By 1920 the Government of Ireland Act provided for two Parliaments in Ireland, one in Belfast and one in Dublin. But Southern Ireland continued to be governed from Westminster and after much fighting and protracted discussions a Treaty was arranged giving dominion status to the twenty-six counties of Southern Ireland under the title Saorstat Eireann (Irish Free State). Although on 14 December 1921 the Dail Eireann voted sixty-four in favour and fifty-seven against, the Republicans continued the fight and from the date of its actual inauguration, 6 December 1922, the Irish Free State ceased to be part of the United Kingdom.

All this led to the formation of the Currency Commission which introduced Irish Free State notes (**32**) for the new government. They are extremely attractive, showing a portrait of Lady Lavery engraved by one of the world's finest engravers, John Harrison, and printed by Waterlow and Sons. The reverses show superb engravings of the famous River Masks. It is noteworthy that there was no obligation on the Dublin authorities to redeem them in Dublin; the notes state: 'Payable to bearer on demand in London'. This was to inspire confidence in the issue and both Irish and English languages were used on the notes.

Collectors should look for the scarcer war-time codes found on some of these notes. Overprinted code-letters in a circle are found at the top left-hand side and bottom right-hand side of each note from 1940 to 1942. At that time the notes, printed in England, had to be shipped across to Ireland in the face of severe enemy attacks on merchant shipping. The codes were intended to keep track of all shipments. The Currency Commission Lady Lavery notes were in use from 1928 to 1942, when the Commission became the Central Bank of Ireland, issuing its first notes in 1943, still with the portrait of Lady Lavery.

At the time of the formation of the Irish Free State there were eight major banking establishments in Southern Ireland, six of them with note-issuing rights. The Currency Commission decided to introduce Consolidated notes for all banks in Southern Ireland. They were admitted as shareholders of the Currency Commission on payment of certain dues and the well-known 'Ploughman series' came into being, depicting a ploughman at work with his team of horses.

Three banks, the Hibernian, the Munster and Leinster, and the Royal, found that under this arrangement they had the right, for the first time, to issue banknotes – and took it. So identically designed notes can be found with eight different bank names on them. With the formation of the Central Bank of Ireland the notes continued to have dual language until 1977 when the English language was dropped altogether. Later the denominations were also changed, to punts.

The notes of Northern Ireland do not have the Irish language upon them at all and are very varied in design and colour, though many of the bank names are the same as those of Southern Ireland. Banks with note issues are: Allied Irish Banks Ltd.; Bank of Ireland (**33**); Belfast Banking Co Ltd, which sold off its branches in the Free State to the Royal Bank of Ireland in 1923; National Bank Ltd; Northern Bank Ltd (**34**), Provincial Bank of Ireland Ltd, and Ulster Bank Ltd (**35**).

Collectors of Irish notes divide them into three sections;

33 Bank of Ireland, Belfast, issue for Northern Ireland in 1942, with the design of Hibernia with harp and the row of heads first introduced by the bank in 1849.

34 Northern Bank Ltd, £5 Belfast issue in 1943. A large number of uncirculated notes from this series were found in an Irish Post Office after the war and have come on to the market.

Northern Ireland, Irish Free State, and the issues of Ireland before the partition. There were fourteen banks issuing notes, some as early as 1870, prior to the partition, and many of these are extremely rare. There are also many provincial banknote issues, some with portraits of William IV. These notes have not been studied in any depth and while it is known that over a

35 Ulster Bank Ltd, £5 Belfast issue of 1940. Notice that many Irish notes of this late period were still handsigned.

---

hundred private banks issued, including some extraordinary denominations, very little is known about them.

In this category are the notes of the Irish Republic issued in 1866 and 1867. These were really bonds and were the product of the Fenian Brotherhood which formed in 1858 from Irish emigrants embittered by English policy towards Ireland. Their leader, who signed some of the notes, was John O'Mahony.

Isle of Man

The small Isle of Man with its population of around 70,000 has a long history of paper money issues. From the ninth century to 1266 it was controlled by the Vikings, until the Scots moved in. It was given by the British Crown to the Earls of Derby and came to be inherited by the Duke of Athol. The island was bought back from him by the British Crown in 1765. To this day the Isle of Man has its own legislative council, the Tynwald of Norse origin, one of the oldest in the world.

The earliest known note is the unissued £5 dated 1 January 1788 of the Isle of Man Bank founded by Taubman and Kennedy, though there is some doubt if this particular enterprise ever actually started up in business. By 1817 there was considerable over-issue of notes, particularly the fractional issues known as 'card notes'. This resulted in an Act of 1817 which had the effect of abolishing all card notes under £1, requiring them to be redeemed by 1 October 1817, after which they were to be invalid. At the same time it ordered all note-issuers to apply for a licence, renewable each year. Fortunately for collectors, the Isle of Man note issues have been studied in depth by Ernest Quarmby in *Banknotes and Banking in the Isle of Man 1788–1970* published by Spink and Son Ltd, which lists all known notes.

English banks which had no right of issue on the mainland were able to obtain licences and issue their own notes. These include Martins Bank Ltd, who trace their history back to 1563, when Sir Thomas Gresham formed a goldsmith business on the site of the present Martins Bank in Lombard Street, London. In those days banking organisations used signs to indicate their business and the Grasshopper, used by the Gresham goldsmiths, appears on the Isle of Man notes of this bank. Lloyds Bank issued notes for the Isle of Man from 1919 to 1961, and these too bear the sign of the banking house, the Black Horse emblem. Lloyds also used a Viking ship to recall the Norse origins of the islanders. Barclays Bank, who had produced many notes for overseas territories, also issued distinctive notes in the Isle of Man from 1924 to 1960. The 1960 dates are extremely rare as most of the printing was destroyed when the licence to issue was revoked. Other English banks included the Lancashire and Yorkshire Bank, Westminster Bank and the Mercantile Bank of Lancashire. All notes issued by these English banks are scarce.

In 1961 the Manx Government decided to issue its own notes, and with the passing of the Isle of Man Government Notes Act of that year, all licences held by commercial banks in the Island were revoked.

The new notes bore a portrait by Annigoni of Queen Elizabeth II and the three legs – the Triune – with the motto 'Quocunque Jeceris Stabit' (whatever way you throw me I shall stand). There are many varieties, like the small and large signature of Stallard. In 1969 the denominations changed to the decimal system and more recently the Isle of Man introduced a plastic pound note, the second territory in the world to do so. Haiti was the first to issue plastic notes, but has since reverted to normal paper. The plastic notes are virtually indistinguishable from normal issues until one feels them, and they have the advantage that they will not tear. Because of their obvious advantage in durability over paper it was at one time thought that many nations would take up the idea. But it appears that the area of plastic notes is something of a forger's paradise, so the main note-issuing authorities decided to retain security paper.

During World War II the Isle of Man was used to house 'enemy aliens' then resident in the United Kingdom. Plans were made to house 13,000 such people and some towns like Port Erin were enclosed as internment camps by wire fencing. The luckless natural inhabitants had to obtain special passes to leave their own town! The number diminished with the setting up of the War Tribunal, which quickly found that most of the 'enemy aliens' were fanatically anti-Nazi and pro-British; and in some cases had relatives in German concentration camps. The note issues for these camps form an interesting study and are very scarce. Major issues were made for the Metropole, Onchan and Peveril. Some were headed 'Civilian Internment Camps'. Internees were allowed to work outside the camps at the rate of 3s.6d. for men and 1s.6d. for women, for which they received the camp notes. Many of the inmates were refugees from Germany, Italians and Finns, but the camp at Peel was for British and foreign Fascists.

Channel Islands

Dependencies of the British Crown, the Channel Islands were the only part of the British Isles to be occupied by Germany in World War II. Their history of banknote issues is long and interesting.

Guernsey did not issue a £1 note until 1808 when the Bank of Guernsey and the Brock Le Mesurier opened. Three years later both banks closed and these notes are extremely rare. When the islanders decided to build the Torteval Church and Jerbourg Monument, the States of Jersey issued their own notes to facilitate the work in 1816; the notes were redeemed in 1818. Then in 1827 private banks began to operate in Guernsey. One of these, the Guernsey Banking Company, became an important bank with a wide circulation extending as far as Cherbourg. States issues gradually took over and in 1914 fractional notes of five and ten shillings were issued. All these early notes are difficult to find and the first notes which are easily obtained are the

German occupation issues of 1941. Guernsey issued 6*d.*, 1*s.*, 1*s.*3*d.*, 2*s.*6*d.*, and 5*s.* denominations. There are many varieties including a rare printing of the 6*d.* made on 1 January 1942 on French blue paper.

Towards the end of the war the islanders began preparing a £1 note and this was actually printed with German personnel in the printing room not realising what was going on. The consequence was that the moment the Germans left the islanders were able to put their own banknotes into circulation. They received a commendation from the Bank of England for being the first occupied territory to resume normal banking. As German notes were widely used in the island they were honoured by the British authorities and for a time advertisements appeared in local newspapers telling the islanders that they could exchange the German notes at the rate of 2*s.* per Reichsmark.

Jersey has a much older history of note-issue, with notes appearing as early as 1797, issued by a wine merchant, Hugh Godrey. In the nineteenth century there were literally hundreds of note-issuing banks, businesses, and individuals, and failures began to occur. Legislation was brought in to prevent the issue of all notes below £1 denomination – there were even notes in livre denominations. In 1817 there were over a hundred different organisations issuing notes. Very few of these notes ever turn up on the market and it would seem that although there were many issuing authorities they were limited in the number of notes they produced.

Like Guernsey, Jersey had its own occupation notes, and these are very popular among collectors because they were designed by the famous artist Edmund Blampied, born in Jersey in 1886. They have very distinctive designs relating to local people and produce.

8
Counterfeit Notes

Early British forgeries

In the early 1800s, British law was not over-much concerned with 'knowingly' being in possession of a forgery, which is the criterion today, but just being in possession was enough. The minimum penalty was transportation and the more usual penalty was a public hanging. That someone who by ill-chance received forged notes could be hanged, seemed unjust to many people, and the Society of Arts published a book in 1819, *Report on the Mode of Preventing the Forgery of Banknotes*, in an attempt to remedy the situation. By this time charges of forgery were so commonplace that juries began to bring in verdicts of 'not guilty' against the clearest evidence, because of the severity of the punishment. The Society of Arts condemned the Bank of England for not taking sufficient trouble to make their notes inimitable and urged a banknote which would defeat the forger.

Notes were at the time produced from copper plates which would each account for about 6,000 notes. With a daily issue of more than 30,000 small notes, this meant a daily consumption of five plates and a total of 1,500 a year. The Society proposed that steel plates should be used, and that only superior artists should be employed, in an attempt to reduce the number of people capable of forging the notes, as at this time copperplate letter writing was a large industry and many people able to make perfect facsimilies.

The book had little or no effect on the Directors of the Bank of England and people continued to hang. But the seeds of reform had been sown, and in about 1826 the famous artist (and reformer) George Cruikshank caused such a stir with his 'anti-hanging note' (**36**) that he succeeded where many eminent minds had failed – and the penalty of hanging for possessing forged banknotes, together with hanging for all minor offences, was abolished for good.

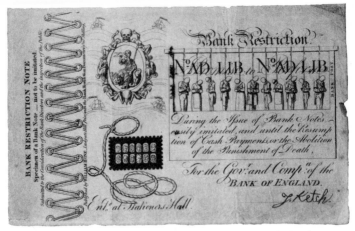

36 Cruikshank's anti-hanging note which drew attention to the harsh punishment for passing forged notes.

Bank of England forgeries

Strangely enough the Bank of England has itself been concerned with the forgery of notes, albeit with Government sanction. The earliest known forgeries are those of French assignats made with a view to ruining the French economy – not that the assignats needed any help from England to become worthless through inflation.

During 1793 the Vendean armies at one time looked like being able to over-power the Republican regime and rumours spread that if they won, only the Royal assignats (those bearing the portrait of Louis XVI), would be redeemed. This led to the Royal assignats appreciating in value while the Republican notes continued to lose value. In fact the Royalist notes were being forged as well as the Republican issues. Most of them were printed in England, with Prime Minister Pitt's approval and they were supplied to the royalist emigrés who attempted an invasion at Quiberon. A large hoard of these forged notes were captured by General Hoche and fear that there may have been many more was probably one of the reasons the notes were demonetised on 15 July 1795.

The Bank of England was also instrumental in forging notes of the Continental Congress in the American War of Independence. These had a more marked effect and were clearly done on a fairly large scale. Indeed the British took out an advertisement in the New York Gazette and the Weekly Mercury on 14 April 1777 during the occupation of New York City by British forces. The advertisement read: 'Persons going into other Colonies may be supplied with any number of counterfeit Congress-Notes, for the price of the paper per ream. They are so neatly and exactly executed that there is no Risque in getting them off, it being almost impossible to discover, that they are not genuine. This has been proved by Bills to a very large Amount, which have already been successfully circulated. Enquire for Q.E.D. at the Coffee House, from 11 p.m to 4 a.m during the present month.'

This advertisement was brought to the notice of George Washington who commented 'no artifices are left untried by the Enemy to injure us'. It should be noted that both the French and the American forgeries are worth more to collectors today than are the originals.

German forgeries of British notes in World War II

The story of the German forgery of British white notes in World War II is stranger than fiction. Something like nine million notes of varying denominations, totalling more than £130 million, were produced. The magnitude of the undertaking did not become apparent until the war was nearly over.

Two events brought the matter to light. A British General got up one morning and saw what seemed to him like half the British army swimming in Lake Toplitz in the freezing winter. He could not believe it and went to investigate. He found a floating bank. The soldiers were diving in and fishing out millions of white Bank of England notes.

At about the same time and not far away, on the Austrian border, a senior German officer found himself looking down the gun-barrels of some American combat troops. They bundled him into a jeep with some other prisoners to send to a prisoner of war camp – but they hurriedly got him back when someone examined the vehicle the officer had been travelling in. It was full of boxes of Bank of England notes. The British Secret Service were called in and the investigation was given top priority – the same rating as capturing the German leaders. Officials at the Bank of England were going whiter than their notes.

Investigations led the British to the village of Redl Zipf where they found the machinery used to print the notes. They never found the plates. Although the investigators were told the forgers had been exterminated at the Ebensee camp, further investigation showed that they had got away, and some were soon tracked down. The most important was Oska Skala, the chief bookkeeper of the whole exercise; and in the spring of 1945 he had unobtrusively got himself a job selling beer when British agents walked into a bar at Pilsen and arrested him.

In charge of the whole operation was an SS Major, Frederick Walter Bernhard Kruger, on the staff of Reichsführer Heinrich Himmler, whose office 6–F–4 devised the scheme for the purpose of ruining Britain's wartime economy. The operation was named 'Bernhard' after him. Instead of having his 'crew' exterminated he had released them (over a hundred) and most survived the war. Kruger was eventually captured. He was never prosecuted but was held by the British for three years and then by the French for a further two. The French, incidentally, offered him the position of head of their department for counterfeiting passports, etc. He declined, and lived in Switzerland until 1981 when he developed lung cancer.

Major Kruger was not the type to make an impression on the aristocratic Prussian officials of the Reichsbank. They disliked the SS, and one Reichsbank President made the mistake of saying so openly, for which he was sent to Theresienstadt Concentration Camp. So Kruger decided to do the job without them. He rounded up all the convicted forgers he could find, about three hundred, and set them to work. Among them was Solomon Smolianoff, a Russian Jew, whose skill as an engraver was equal to the top world engravers of his day.

One of the compounds at Sachenhausen Concentration Camp was shrouded in secrecy and to anyone who asked it was simply called 'Barracks 19'. Here the printing machines churned out British notes. To print notes which would fool experts required equipment capable of applying the necessary pressure. To produce the correct 'feel' required approximately two hundred tons of pressure, which forces the paper into the recesses of the plate where it picks up the ink. On drying, a lovely crisp relief print is formed. The counterfeiter working in a back room has a great deal of difficulty solving that problem. But not Kruger, who had the resources of Germany at his disposal, as the correct machinery existed in industrial Germany. The ink was no problem at all, but getting the paper right was the major headache. From 1724 the Bank of England had contracted Henry Portal to become its sole papermaker – and Portals supply the paper to this day. Nevertheless the Germans made a good job of it. Experts say that under careful analysis the German paper is shown to be harder, a bit glossier and whiter than the real thing, and that it also makes a different rustling noise when handled. Smolianoff was not deceived by the devices incorporated into the genuine notes by the Bank of England to catch an ordinary counterfeiter. There are various items, like a little white scratch half way down the 'i' of the 'Five', a nick in the 'f' of 'Compa. of the'. Smolianoff faithfully copied them all.

The British were on the lookout for forgeries and within a year, 1943, were on to them. The Germans expected it. What the British did not realise was that the Germans were producing various different grades of forgery. They effectively stopped looking after they had detected several types. The top grade escaped their inspection. Indeed some of the top grade notes were given to a Swiss bank with instructions to check them. The notes were shown to a Bank of England official who passed them. Only later when quantities became available did they take a closer look and find minute differences.

In the meantime the Germans used the notes for paying collaborators and agents in neutral countries, among them the famous spy 'Cicero', who gave the Germans the correct Allied Invasion Plans, although they did not realise it, because of the many 'invasion plans' which were deliberately being 'leaked' by the British. Many of the notes were stored, with the intention of dropping them over Britain to disrupt the economy.

Himmler was delighted at the progress and wanted to do the same with American notes. Kruger was delighted too, but for a different reason. He told his men: 'Slow down. If you complete the job too soon I will be sent to the Russian front and you will be executed'. The authorities would not want any 'living' evidence of the operation.

And so it was that Kruger's men were still working on the project when gunfire reached the camp precincts. They chose their moment and bolted; it was March 1945. They had forged other notes besides the famous White Fiver; £10, £20, £50, £100, £500 and £1000. The £20 and £50 exist in far greater quantities than is generally realised, with both Peppiatt and Catterns signatures. Provincial Bank 'handstamps' were also put on the backs of some of the forged notes to give them greater authenticity. It is believed they had also produced a good $100 USA note although no examples of it are known in private hands. Some of the white £5 forgeries can still be bought in Italy for as little as £3 to £5, but it is an offence in the United Kingdom to 'knowingly be in possession' of a forged Bank of England note.

The Germans made a number of errors which experts can detect. These are listed in the 1945 *Czechoslovakian Report*, based on information supplied by Skala. The simplest of these is the watermark error. If you look at the first 'n' of 'England', in the words 'Bank of England' in the watermark, you will see a faint curved line leading down from the triangular 'toe' of the first limb of 'n', to the bottom of the watermark. If that line is slightly to the left of centre of the 'toe' it is likely to be genuine. If it starts from the centre it is a German forgery. The Bank of England will not 'divulge our sources of counterfeit detection', but as far as we know this method of detection is the most reliable.

The Bank of Portugal

The most audacious forgery of banknotes of all time must surely be the affair of the Bank of Portugal. Behind the scheme was Arthur Virgilio Alves Reis. What he did was simply to forge documents requiring the printers to print notes for him. He had a plausible gang of suitably notable gentlemen who were able to impress Sir William Waterlow of the famous printing house, Waterlow and Sons.

Effectively they told him that the printing order was in great secrecy, and much more business would follow. There were political problems and the notes would be overprinted in Portugal for use in Angola. That they suceeded in convincing Sir William is shown by the great pains he went to in order to prevent fellow directors learning about the order. The most incredible fact of all is that the printed notes were put in suitcases and left at the left-luggage office in Liverpool Street Station! Even more astounding, the forgers went back for a second helping!

Of course the Bank of Portugal soon became suspicious that something was up. There were far too many 500 escudo notes about; but examine them as they would, nothing appeared to be wrong. They were perfect and had to have been printed from the original plates; and no forger can reproduce that to fool microscopic examination. It was a bank teller named de Sousa, working for a money-changer, who first told the authorities that the notes were forged. As a result of that a guard was put round the Bank of Angola and Metropole and the branch manager, Adriano Silva, was arrested in the street and packed off to prison. Then came the massive search of the money-changers and the jewellery shop next door, in both of which quantities of mint 500 escudo notes were found. But as the day wore on the investigators became increasingly concerned, as all the notes were perfect, and they had gone in without search warrants, imprisoned people, and now had to justify it all.

One of the bank officials present at the search, Campos e Sa, suddenly noticed something very unusual. The notes were not in consecutive order and, being contained in packets, they would have been if they had come from the Bank of Portugal. A minute examination was carried out of all the notes and the next day the investigators found their first duplication of numbers on the notes. Now they knew that they were forgeries.

It was only when the Bank of Portugal then got in touch with Waterlow's that the whole story unravelled itself. Just how close Reis came to getting away with it is shown by the fact that he had nearly bought, through his intermediaries, enough shares of the Bank of Portugal to take control. Then he and his colleagues would have been in a position to destroy the incriminating evidence. The whole story of this quite fantastic episode is found in 'The Man who Stole Portugal' by Murray Teigh Bloom, published by Secker and Warburg.

Forged notes are often worth much more than the genuine issues, but collectors need to be careful that they are not breaking the law in collecting certain items. It is an offence to be knowingly in possession of a forged British banknote in the UK.

Propaganda notes

There is another type of forgery, not intended to deceive, but to draw attention to itself. This is the propaganda note; and usually one side is an exact copy of a currency-note while the other carries propaganda. During World War II both sides produced many such propaganda notes. It is possible to make an enormous collection of such items.

Germany forged the current issue £1 note of the 1940 period but were not over-concerned about its exactness as the colour is more grey-black than green. But on the back they put a message which was in fact quite prophetic, informing the British that the empire was about to fall to pieces and that the money would be worthless. Two varieties of this note are known.

The British found a way of getting their propaganda directly to the German soldier. The efficient Germans had introduced a special type of military currency for their soldiers. If it was spent in military establishments it was worth ten times the face value. If it was spent in the local town it was only worth the face value, so the system ensured that soldiers spent the money in camp. The British forged the notes, which were uniface, and used the blank side for propaganda. The first two types were written in the form of poetry. One says: (translated), 'My name is 50 pfennig. I'll cheat everyone out of 4.50 who believes Hitler will give him anything'.

Another starts with the line 'Ich bin Hitlers Arschwiesch' which reads in a more sensitive translation, 'I am a piece of Hitler's toilet paper. Nobody accepts me because nobody can buy anything with me'.

The scarcest of these propaganda notes, all on 'Behelfs-zahlungsmittel fur die Deutsche Wehrmacht', is a long message of which only 2,800 were distributed during Operation Durham in the Trondheim area in 1944.

It reads: 'This bill is a farce – just as the war is. With this piece of toilet paper, they want to pay for the soldiers' blood – Soldiers' blood which carries on the war – the war which is continued only so that the big shots can get their loot out of the country. The high ranking officers, SS Big Shots, the Party grafters and the trustees can obtain as much hard currency as they want. With that, they can buy and send home anything they want. They live high on the hog in their illegal private clubs and can afford to pay fantastic prices for their food. But the troops only get this concentration camp money which they can only spend in canteens. The troops have to eat whatever the canteens want to get rid of because they can't spend this paper anywhere else. This bill is a farce, a bad cheque which can't be cashed – Just as everything else which we have been promised. End the War. End this farce.' Yet another note of the same type contains two of the 'poems' on the same note.

Many of the Japanese occupation notes were forged by the British with suitable propaganda, using the local script and intended to be understood even by the partly educated. A typical translation is: 'Here is a word of advice about money. British money is good money. British Burma banknotes are good. India small coin and India notes are good. British military adminstration notes are good. But beware of Japanese imitations made to look like good money. Remember all forms of Japanese currency are bad. British money is good money, Japanese money is worthless'.

Chinese engravers working under the Japanese occupation produced a variety of propaganda messages, more subtly hidden so that the Japansese would not notice them too quickly. The 200 yuan note of the Central Reserve Bank can be found with four initial letters in different parts of the note, USAC standing for 'United States Army Coming'. The 50 cent notes of the same bank, with three different colour varieties, have the letters CGWRS 'Central Government will return soon'. Other notes have designs of half turtles or wolves in the margin. To the Chinese to be called an 'egg of a turtle' is like being called a bastard. The wolf is regarded as an emblem of rapaciousness. Other notes have ancient Chinese worthies making obscene gestures.

The world of propaganda clearly had its successes as the use of such material was carried on into the Korean war and the Vietnam war. Banknote designs were also commonly used to attract attention to leaflets dropped over enemy lines which were in effect Surrender Passes, promising good treatment to those who used them.

9
Paper Money at War

The earliest known paper money of Europe came about as a result of war. When a town was besieged it had little to offer its defenders except promises to pay later. In some instances, of course, towns kept going for a while with silver and gold. During the Civil War in England, Newark, Pontefract and Scarborough cut up silver plate and issued it as coin. But this was not always possible. When the Moors put the town of Alhama in Granada under siege in 1483, the commander of the beleaguered garrison, the Conde de Tendilla, produced paper notes in the name of the King of Aragon promising to pay the equivalent sum in gold or silver after the siege was raised. These were probably the first European paper money though none has survived.

During the siege of Leyden in 1572, the citizens cut up book bindings (including Bibles), embossed them with an official mark and used them as coins. Strips of leather money were used when the Turks besieged Belgrade in 1688, and similar leather notes were used in 1716 by the Danes when they were besieged in Oslo by the Swedes.

The convenience to a nation at war of issuing paper money instead of coin was not lost on the authorities and before long paper money was being issued in vast quantities and far in excess of the issuers' ability to back it by coin. During the French Revolution there were various siege notes which collectors look for today. The French Royalists who held the city of Lyons against the Republicans for two months in 1793 issued notes with the heading: 'Lyons Besieged – Resistance to Oppression'. Later in the same year Republican troops found themselves trapped in the city of Mayence (Mainz) by the advancing Prussian army and they issued paper money for five sols to fifty livres.

Sometimes the war-notes of a country were also the first issues of paper money for that country. This was the case for Poland in 1794. Tadeusz Kosciuszko led a rebellion, unique in history as it was supported by rich and poor alike. The insurrection started with considerable success when his army of mixed peasants and regulars put a Russian army of veterans to flight at Raclawice, but later battles crushed the insurrection. Kosciuszko notes are still sometimes found and remain a testimony to a great man of freedom.

At Colberg it was the Prussians' turn to be besieged by the French in 1807. They issued various kinds of notes; commission coupons authorised by the Coinage Commission and the Meinecke notes, named after the Counsellor for War and Crown Lands.

When the French were besieged in Erfurt by the Prussians in 1813, the French Commander issued siege notes printed in the German language. The year 1848 was the Year of the Revolutions when popular uprisings occurred in Europe against oppressive government. Hungary was in revolt against the Hapsburgs and issued notes at Esseg, Komarom and Temesvar. A series of notes inscribed 'Moneta Patriottica' were issued by Italians under siege at Venice by the Austrians, in the same year. Several Italian groups in Lombardo-Venezia also issued notes completely handwritten, others printed.

Among the most interesting of the many issues of war money in 1848 are the notes of Lajos Kossuth of Hungary. Many of these are still easily available to collectors and are reminders of great historical events. Hungarian patriot, champion of liberty, and president of the first Hungarian Republic during the War of Independence in 1848, Kossuth was forced into exile. He issued notes in England and the United States to raise funds for a return to Hungary, where he was confident of revolutionary support. The revolution never came about and many of the notes have survived.

Before his exile Kossuth made a number of issues in Hungary, known as *Kamatos utalvany* (interest-bearing legal tender treasury bills). But it was his exile notes that caused a sensation. Indirectly they led to the downfall of Lord Palmerston. When Kossuth came to England in 1851 he was received with great enthusiasm, but the political repercussions were serious. The Austrian Government had been deeply offended by an attack on General Haynaw of Austria at Barclay's Brewery in September 1850, and particularly by an unconciliatory note from Palmerston on the matter. They regarded Kossuth's reception in England as hostile to Austria. When it was known that Palmerston was going to receive Kossuth, the Austrian Ambassador threatened to leave the country. Lord John Russell prevented the interview and the whole matter was eventually made one of the charges of independent action brought against Palmerston which caused his dismissal in 1852.

Nevertheless, Kossuth, impressed with his reception by the British, came back in 1860 and issued notes in the English language for his cause. The Emperor of Austria promptly complained to the British Government and soldiers were sent round to the printers to destroy the notes and plates. Only a handful have survived. Two of the known notes were the property of the foreman-printer who had the right to two examples of all notes printed by his firm, and had taken them home before the troops arrived.

The Confederate States

One very popular field among collectors of war paper money is the Confederate States. There was only one small steel plate engraving firm in the whole of the South when the Confederates, with much patriotic fervour, unfurled their banners of war. Attempts were made to organise the printing of notes in the North in the months before the declaration of war. Negotiations were carried out through a sympathiser of the South with the National Banknote Company and on 2 April 1861, only ten days before the outbreak of war, a shipment of notes was sent to the South. It comprised 607 sheets of $50, $100, $500, and $1,000 denominations, all of which are now rare. Oddly, the $1,000 has portraits of John C. Calhoun, a patriotic Southerner, and Andrew Jackson, 'The Union, it must be preserved'!

The North did not wake up to what was happening until 22 April when Federal Marshals moved in with force and confiscated the printing plates. The Confederacy, which had always had ninety per cent of its paper currency printed in the North, were now in deep trouble. Banks were asked to hand over any unused plates so that they could be converted to Confederate notes. One printer, Jules Manouvrier, seemed able to produce first-class printed notes, but a large theft of his finished work shook the Confederate officials. They recovered the notes, but when they tried to find out how many had been put into circulation by the thieves, they found that the printer literally had no idea of how many he had printed. His contract was cancelled and the notes burned.

Prominent printers were Hoyer and Ludwig, a small lithographic firm in Richmond. But they were quite unable to keep up with the demand and the workmanship got worse and worse, so even spelling mistakes occurred. Ludwig's notes looked like counterfeits and the counterfeiters were not slow to realise this. In no time there were thousands of counterfeits and tradesmen began to refuse to accept any note printed by Hoyer and Ludwig. The Secretary of the Treasury finally recalled the notes to exchange them for new ones, but as there were no new notes to give out, he issued call certificates, payable ninety days after issue with interest, while he had new notes printed. Inflation was making things worse and notes began to appear 'with interest at 2 cents a day' to try and make them more popular.

The quality of paper had been steadily deteriorating and when the paper mill at Bath in South Carolina burned down in 1862 the South had no option but to resort to blockade running. Shipments of paper were sent from England and some of them were captured by the North. It was not until 1864 that the South was again able to produce enough of its own paper.

The printers themselves were often at loggerheads and one printer, Blanton Duncan, sent men round to burn down Keatinge, another printing firm. Duncan had produced the famous 'Sweet Potato Dinner' note, which shows a scene from the American Revolution when Marion entertained the British Officer Tarleton to discuss an exchange of prisoners. His negro servant prepared a seven course meal, all based on the sweet potato, trying to give the British the impression that there was no food shortage. But Keatinge had taken the precaution of having armed men on the premises and the attack was driven off.

Duncan had his own problems when soldiers who had been seconded to him for use as printers, took time off to go to the local brothels. Duncan went to the Provost Marshal for help as the Columbia Garrison depended on the printing firm for their wages. The Marshal showed no interest until it was pointed out that this meant that he too was unlikely to be paid. The Garrison was then turned out and rounded up the errant printers.

The main problem facing the collector is the large number of counterfeit notes. But it should be remembered that these are contemporary forgeries and as such, well worth a place in a collection of Confederate notes. Identifying many of them is hard simply because the correct notes were also badly printed. All these notes were hand-signed by two people and the authorities shared the work out among many signers who were given batches of notes each. Fortunately for collectors, records were kept of these so that today we know which signature combinations should appear with which serial numbers – a fact not known to contemporary counterfeiters, who were facing the proverbial task of finding a needle in a haystack to get the right combination by chance. This information can be found in *Register of the Confederate Debt* by Raphael P. Thian, which tables all signatories and numbers.

The last issue of the Confederate notes, dated 17 February 1864 at Richmond, has some twenty varieties in nine note types. Some of these are very rare yet few European dealers even appreciate that there are so many varieties. Although dated 1864, a printing of the $500 (picturing General 'Stonewall' Jackson) was made in 1865. General Sherman burned Columbia in February 1865 and the plates were smuggled out to Richmond where Ludwig ran off some 5,000 sheets before the Confederates had to evacuate the city. The Confederacy surrendered on 9 April and Confederate notes became worthless. The last printing can easily be distinguished as they are on bright red paper as against the dull red paper of earlier printings.

Siege of Khartoum

A good deal is known about the notes signed by General Gordon at the siege of Khartoum (**37**), thanks to the extensive research carried out by the late Martin Parr who was at one time secretary to Gordon's successor. Very little was known about the Gordon notes until 1929 when H.C. Jackson sent a five piastre note to the Secretary of the Gordon Memorial Fund, suggesting that such notes should be collected and sold on behalf of the Gordon Memorial Fund. The note he sent was in fact a forgery; the number and seal were lithographed instead of being added later, and in place of 'Nigri' there was written 'Yijri'. Martin Parr

37 General Gordon hand-signed notes at Khartoum in 1884 shortly before he was killed by the Mahdi's forces. A 20 piastre note

examined the note and it is amusing to think that it was a dud which caused the resurrection of the notes. For in 1930 Parr started to get on the track of the notes through Samuel Bey Atiya, who stated that the vast majority had been returned to the Egyptian Treasury at the reoccupation, some having been honoured and some not.

Acting for the Governor of the Sudan, Parr wrote on 19 November 1930 to R.E. More, asking him to get the Minister of Finance to locate the notes and let the Governor have them. The correspondence led to a letter from the Egyptian Prime Minister saying he had no objection to the notes being handed over, provided the Egyptian Government were indemnified from any subsequent claim a holder might make. The letter was shown to Sir Robert Creg, British Commissioner of the Caisse de la Dette, who said he could not hand over the notes because the Prime Minister had not given express authorisation to do so. The Prime Minister was approached again on the matter, and permission obtained. The notes were flown to Khartoum, where Martin Parr received them for a thorough examination.

There were 3,800 notes and it was remarkable that an order for their destruction had been given; but the notes had been temporarily lost and escaped the order. They were only found as a result of Parr's persistence. Strangely they were again lost, during the course of World War II. They surfaced again in the United States of America just over a year ago and are now being offered to collectors.

Martin Parr wrote of the notes: 'There is but little need to stress the romance of the Gordon notes. All who are familiar with the story of the Siege of Khartoum know that without money which the defender created by the prestige of his own name, the defence would have collapsed much earlier. The fate of the Gordon notes after the sack of Khartoum and of Sennar, how they were publicly burned, how to possess one was a crime punished condignly and brutally, how they were left in the streets for goats to eat, is all well known. But some were hidden; gradually by devious paths, at the risk of their owners' lives, they made in months or even years the terrible journey across the desert. Hidden in clothing, or at the bottom of grain bags, passed surreptitiously from hand to hand, they reached at last the land of Egypt, where one would have expected them to be honoured in every sense of the word. But instead they were mostly repudiated; after ignominious law-suits and bickerings they passed into oblivion in the vaults of the Cassie de la Dette, an oblivion so complete that they escaped the order for their own destruction.'

The notes examined were:

Denomination	Numbers examined	Lowest serial	Highest serial	Estimated total	Total in Egyptian £
5 PT	39	72	16545	20000	1000
10 PT	184	302	14249	15000	1500
20 PT	423	3	26104	30000	6000
100 PT	1215	9	19948	20000	20000
500 PT	226	13	2000	2000	10000
1000 PT	99	15	991	1000	10000
2000 PT	54	29	498	500	10000
2500 PT	1041	27	1980	2000	50000
5000 PT	193	202	1178	2000	50000
£E 50	12	12	178	200	10000

This, better than anything, gives a collector a guide to the rarity of the issues. It will be noticed that there were very few of any of the denominations except two.

General Gordon wrote in his diary regarding the £50 notes: 'I offered in paying the three months "Backsheesh" to the troops to give orders for bulk sums, £120, £130, but they refused to accept them, as they want regular paper money, so I have issued £10,000 more in £50 notes. In this paper money I am personally responsible for the liquidation and anyone can bring action against me, in my individual capacity, to recover the money, while in the orders it might be a query whether they (the Cairo authorities), might not decline to pay the orders.'

There was a one piastre note, but very few have survived (about four are known). The reason is simply that nobody was prepared to risk his life for one piastre. Unlike the other denominations, the one piastre is a square note and would be easily recognised. The last one that came on the market fetched $3,600.

Gordon sat up night after night hand-signing the notes. An amusing story is told that the people complained that the candle-lights in the Palace were too bright and made a good target for Dervish snipers. Gordon is said to have replied to them that when God distributed fear he came to Gordon and found there was no fear left. But it did take up a lot of time and efforts were made to hectograph the signature to save him the time of hand-signing. The hectograph signature was not acceptable to the townspeople and he had to revert to hand-signing.

Early Gordon notes are on high quality linen and are much scarcer than later issues which are often on cheap Egyptian envelope paper. Some can be found with handstamps on the back indicating their use in court cases fought over redemption.

Boer War

There is much historical paper money relating to the Boer War of 1900 to 1902; a war won by the British, but at the cost of 100,000 lives, far in excess of the total Boer forces. The Boers issued three different types of note. The first, the Pretoria series, were dated 28 May 1900, exactly a week before Lord Roberts occupied the city. The second series was issued at Pietersburg, which became the seat of the Boer government after the fall of Pretoria. The third series are known as the Pilgrims Rest issue or the Te Velde (issued in the Field) issue. They were printed on school-book lined

38 a Mr E.C. Ross producing Mafeking £1 notes by the ferro-prussiate process under siege. He was able to make twenty a day.

b Captain Greener, paymaster, examines the notes at the entrance of the dug-out Standard Bank.

notepaper on a small portable press at the small mining town of Pilgrims Rest in the Eastern Transvaal. The men who printed them were the same who produced the Velde Ponde gold sovereigns. After the war the British repudiated the notes, but they were able to serve as evidence of a War debt and can be found with rubber stamps for 'Central Judicial Commission', etc., as late as 1907. During the fighting a quantity of notes were captured by the British and these were overstamped 'Captured and Cancelled'.

But perhaps the most interesting notes of the Boer War were those of the Siege of Mafeking, defended by Baden-Powell who was to form the Boy Scout Movement later on. The Bank, run by the Standard Bank of South Africa, was a dug-out (**38**) and the problems of printing notes were recorded by Baden-Powell who, referring to the ten-shilling note which shows a soldier with a field gun and another with a Maxim, wrote: 'We tried various dodges, drew a design on copper, bit it out with acid all right, but could not get sufficient pressure to print it, even using a mangle, then we cut a croquet mallet in half and made a woodcut'.

The £1 note (**39**), with its patriotic design of defenders under the Union Jack with the home-made gun, is a rare item, as only 683 were produced, at the rate of twenty a day, by the Ferro Prussiate process. The gun is 'The Wolf', a nickname given to Baden-Powell by the natives who knew him as 'The Wolf that never sleeps'. Most of the notes survived because they were avidly sought immediately the siege was lifted. Indeed, the Mafeking Mail at the end of the siege contained an advertisement selling the notes at several times face value. The rarest of the siege of Mafeking notes is the plain three shillings. One and two shilling notes were also issued.

Postage stamps were also used as currency. When the Boers cut the railway line from the Cape to Bechuanaland, the Government Secretary of Matabeleland, H. Marshall Hole, had specially printed cards bearing his signature issued with postage stamps affixed according to the value of the card-note. Cut off from supplies, Major Birbeck commanding the Upington Border Scouts resorted to a most unusual method of paying his troops. He made notes out of khaki shirt-sleeves, calico and hessian, and even table-cloths. Early ones were totally hand written, but later ones were overstamped 'Issued by Paymaster, B.S. Upington'.

39 A Mafeking siege £1 note picturing the home-made gun named 'Wolf' after Baden-Powell, who was known as 'The Wolf that never sleeps' by the natives. It took 15 minutes to make each note, and a total of 683 were printed.

A siege note was issued in Koffyfontein, a small diamond-mining town near Kimberley, which is very rare, but probably the scarcest of all Boer siege notes are those of O'okiep. These notes were printed on an ordinary office machine. O'okiep was under siege from 4 April to 4 May 1902, and General Smuts, conducting the Boer forces, was called away to negotiate the surrender of all Boer Forces during the siege. The little town in Namaqualand, seventy-five miles from the coast, was the base of the Cape Copper Mining Co. Lieutenant-Colonel Shelton of the 3rd West Surrey Regiment commanded the forces which consisted of 661 half-castes, 206 European miners, 44 men of the 9th Warwickshire Militia and 12 men of the Cape Garrison Artillery. The notes were signed by Captain Macdonald, the Intelligence Officer and by Lieutenant Wood, Paymaster.

40 100 lire note intended for the occupation of the Sudan. Mussolini
personally ordered them to be destroyed when it became apparent his troops
would not be able to occupy the territory.

World War II

The paper money issued during World War II is more than
enough for a specialised collection. In fact many collectors
specialise in certain areas of World War II. There are prisoner-of-
war notes, concentration camp issues, guerilla notes, military
notes, invasion notes and occupation currency. The story of
World War II can be told through its issues of paper money.
Some of the issues proved an embarrassment to the issuers of
paper money. The Italian dictator, Benito Mussolini, prepared
notes of great artistic beauty (**40**) for the occupation of Sudan and
Egypt (the same designs were used in Greece), but when it
became apparent that his forces were not going to get anywhere
near Egypt or the Sudan he personally gave instructions for them
to be destroyed, thus hoping to cover up his embarrassment. A
few survived, and one complete set was kept as a souvenir by the
Minister of Finance. It was subsequently sold to an American
who split the set with another collector.

Perhaps the most embarrassing issue of all, however, was the
1944 'invasion' notes of the Allies (**41**). Carried over the beaches
on D-Day, these had on one side the wording 'Emis En (issued in)
France' and on the reverse the Tricolour of France. General de
Gaulle was furious. He had not been told about their issue until
the last moment and when he saw them he exploded, claiming

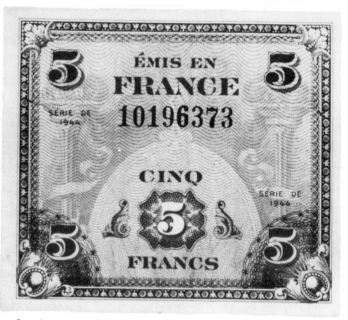

41 Invasion note carried over the beaches on D-Day in 1944. The wording 'Emis en' (issued in) France, caused a political row between General de Gaulle and the British and Americans. He had not been told about the notes, and threatened to have them refused as currency by the French.

vociferously that the notes were an insult because they were not issued in France at all but had been carefully and secretly printed by the Allies, using the American printers, Forbes. More than that, declared de Gaulle, no-one had the right to use the Tricolour except a Frenchman. As his influence on the French Committee of National Liberation (CLN) was so strong, the Allies were faced with the prospect of Underground announcements in France declaring the notes to be invalid. When Eisenhower was told of this possibility he snapped 'To hell with him, issue the notes'. Churchill refers to the incident in his memoirs, and in deference to de Gaulle the next issue of notes did away with the offending words and the Tricolour. Churchill commented that de Gaulle was his Cross of Lorraine!

Even more embarrassing for the Allies was the 5,000 franc

invasion note. Although the issues had been successfully kept secret from the Axis powers, it appears that a well-informed counterfeit organisation was aware of them and got to work right away. Unfortunately for them, they were too quick off the mark, and put the forgeries into circulation before the note was due to be issued. The authorities immediately cancelled the whole issue.

One affair which caused the Italians trouble started when Montenegrin officials fled to the mountains with a convoy of Yugoslavian paper money. They hid the money in caves when the tracks became impassable for vehicles, and continued their flight on foot. Local peasants had watched, and were soon helping themselves, so when the Italian army marched into the territory they were surprised at the enormous wealth of the peasant population. When they found out what had happened, all the notes were called in. From the bank they obtained the serial numbers of the notes which had been hidden in the mountains, and any such notes were confiscated. The others were overstamped with a circular handstamp 'Verificato' (verified) and allowed to circulate. Yugoslav guerillas under Tito had no trouble in forging the 'Verificato' stamp.

When Norway faced the might of Germany early in World War II, Major General Steffens was instructed to hold up the Germans while the King and his cabinet escaped in a British destroyer. Steffens blocked the way at Voss allowing the King to escape and in the process was soon surrounded by German forces. Incredibly, the Germans had not interfered with the telephone system, and Steffens, who considered that all things should be done properly, telephoned the head bank in Bergen and asked for authority to issue emergency paper money for his troops. The somewhat surprised bank officials readily agreed. These notes, bearing the signature of Steffens, are highly prized by collectors today. See (**42**) on p. 122.

During the Warsaw uprising the partisans overprinted Polish notes with patriotic messages and, in one case, a Swastika swinging from a gallows. There were many types of overprint because both capitalist and communist factions issued them. They are identified by the eagle crowned or uncrowned (**43**). Collectors need to be careful with these notes as some were officially reproduced after the war, not to deceive collectors, but as souvenirs of the uprising.

42 The emergency 10 kroner issued by Major General Steffens in 1940 when his forces were surrounded by advancing Germans.

Slovak partisans issued many types of notes, some printed in the woods and bearing the ominous message 'Death to Fascism'. The first war-note of World War II was the Narodowy Bank, Polksi, Warsaw issue, overprinted with an oblique red rectangle for the General Government for occupied Polish Territories. This note has been forged to deceive collectors, but is easy to identify. The forgery is lithographed instead of engraved. Germany was issuing war-notes to within a week of the surrender. The last note which can be reasonably obtained by collectors is the 20 Reichsmark of Sudetenland and Lower Silesia, with the printed date of issue 28 April 1945. The Third Reich surrendered unconditionally one week later.

It has often been said that Hitler turned Germany's armies against Russia on a whim and without enough preparation. But the evidence of paper money shows that there had been long-term planning. Well-printed notes dated 1941, and with the place of issue given as Kiev, were prepared. Specimens of these notes were literally picked up in the street outside the German Reich Printing Works in Berlin after a bombing raid had destroyed the buildings.

Many different types of prisoner-of-war notes were issued by

43 Warsaw Uprising. The Polish forces overprinted circulating banknotes. Most were destroyed when the Germans finally annihilated the ghetto.

44 The 'red-triangle' symbol found on all notes issued by the Germans for use by prisoners-of-war in World War II.

both sides (**44**). Germany also printed concentration camp notes, some of which are now extremely rare. More than 30 major and about 250 minor or temporary concentration camps were set up by the Third Reich. Notes of Theresienstadt and some of the Litzmanstadt issues have survived in large quantities. British combat troops got into Buchenwald before the Germans had time to destroy the notes and these are often available. But apart from those the notes are very rare. In an attempt to destroy all evidence of the camps, the notes were destroyed along with everything else. Consequently the only ones that are available

45 Theresienstadt concentration camp notes for 50 and 100 kronen, dated 1943. The portrait of Moses and the Tablet of the Law was 'doctored' by the SS in Berlin who said the original design was 'too Aryan'.

are generally those which were in possession of survivors. Notes from the extermination camps usually fetch more than £250 because of their scarcity.

One issue of notes from the concentration camp of Theresienstadt have an unusual history. At first the elders of the camp were invited to design the notes, which they did, showing Moses and the Tablet of the Law. But the SS in Berlin took exception to the 'Aryan' features of Moses and altered them to look more like Fagin (**45**). When the Jewish people in the camp refused to use the notes the Germans brought in a tax on free time, which had to be paid in these notes, thus enforcing their circulation.

The subject of World War II paper money is vast and interested collectors are well advised to get a copy of *World War II Military Currency* by C. Frederick Schwan and Joseph E. Boling, which lists all known issues and gives many of the stories behind the notes.

Other wartime issues

When the State of Israel was formed, an issue of notes was made on what was virtually a wartime footing. The British clearly were not putting themselves out, on relinquishing mandate authority, to leave a workable banking system; but some far-sighted Israel bankers saw the problems coming and sent E.L. Hoofien to negotiate in secret for special printings of notes to be put into circulation the day the British left. He encountered enormous problems, as no major international security printer was prepared to undertake what was effectively a 'pirate' issue as long as the British were still in control. Theoretically such an issue would be backed by the British which would have given the printers a legal problem under international law.

The problem was solved by replacing the legal tender clause – which appears on the Specimen notes – by the wording 'The bank will accept this note for payment in any account' (normally it would be 'for the payment of any amount'). Such a statement was of course meaningless. The American Banknote Co. then agreed to print them and in great secrecy the consignment was flown by Royal Dutch Airlines to a temporary airfield in the north of Israel, as Lod was already in Arab hands, and from there they were taken by armoured cars to Haifa. They arrived in Tel Aviv in July 1948 and were issued on 18 August of that year, the day the British left.

A bandit chief, Pancol Villa of Mexico, once issued his own notes, during the Mexican civil war. Styling himself 'General Francisco Villa' he ordered superbly engraved notes from American printers. When they arrived he was highly delighted, but his advisers pointed out that the notes had spaces for signatures and that they somehow had to be signed. Villa, not

46 An 1865 2 peso note of Paraguay.

noted for his literary abilities, decided this was unnecessary and ordered that the notes should be put into circulation without signatures. Much rarer are the notes of a compatriot of his, Zapata, who had formed a coalition with Villa. The southern and central states of Mexico which came under Zapata's control were existing on masses of cardboard notes, in which the public had no confidence. Zapata's forces instituted the Banco Revolucionario de Guerrero and banknotes were issued in 1914. But no bank was ever actually opened. The notes circulated without any backing and with nowhere to go to redeem them. It is probable that Zapata intended to build a bank but he was betrayed by Carranza when invited to attend a conference to negotiate a settlement. A guard of honour presented arms upon his arrival and bugles sounded a call of honour. As he marched up to the entrance of the building the Guard of Honour, previously instructed, shot him dead with a volley.

In Cuba, Dr Fidel Castro issued a decree on 5 August 1961 invalidating all circulating notes on 7 August. As 5 August was a Saturday it meant that no-one had time to do anything about it! He appointed Dr Che Guevara as President of the National Bank and he signed Cuban banknotes with his nickname 'Che'. Quite how Guevara was chosen as president of a bank is not known, but an amusing story circulated that Castro had asked among his friends: 'Who is a good economist among you?' Che Guevara had put his hand up and was made President of the Bank. Afterwards he told his friends: 'I thought he asked, who is a good communist among you?'!

One issue of war-notes is still common today for the simple reason that very few people survived to spend any of the notes at the time. These are the issues of Paraguay (**46**), whose neighbours decided to settle the border disputes once and for all with an invasion in 1865. Five years of bloody war killed more than three-quarters of the population. Every able-bodied man was pressed into war-service and battalions were formed from twelve-year-old boys and women. Over a million were killed in battle and, with the death of Lopez, the nation finally surrendered. There were less than 30,000 men in the country alive.

10

Art on Banknotes

Early banknotes were plain, simple and issued for short duration to meet emergencies. Only when banknotes began to dominate the financial world in the nineteenth century did printers begin to vie with each other to produce beautiful and intricately designed notes (**47, 48**). As counterfeiters became more competent, security printing firms became even more skilled at note production in order to keep ahead.

The result is that modern banknotes are miniature works of art in their own right. The world's greatest engravers are employed to produce them; not to please collectors, but to defeat counterfeiters. The end product, however, is a minor masterpiece well worth collecting for its own sake. More collectors are turning to the 'art' side of banknotes; a field which has been neglected, but which is full of surprises. For instance, most people do not realise that it takes about six months to engrave a banknote plate, that sometimes two or three engravers work on the same plate, that there are less than a dozen top class security engravers in Europe today, and that it can take twenty-five years to train a top class portrait engraver.

The use of several engravers on the same plate is partly to speed up production, but mainly to make the counterfeiters task even more difficult. Engravers, like all artists, develop their own styles and with a little practice a collector can often identify the work of a particular engraver. It is hard enough for a forger to copy *one*, let alone the styles of three different experts. There are only a handful of major security printers throughout the world; for example Bradbury, Wilkinson Plc., and the American Bank Note Co. They are always on the lookout for engraving talent, but they have to plan ahead, for it literally takes years and years of training. It is not just artistic skill that these firms are looking for, but that certain type of mind that can exercise an extraordinary degree of patience, steadiness and concentration over long

47 Swedish private bank 100 kronor of 1874 and Sarawak Government $50 with a portrait of C. Vyner Brooke, both engraved by Bradbury Wilkinson Plc.

48 Early Egyptian notes engraved by Bradbury Wilkinson Plc for the National Bank of Egypt. The £10 features sailing vessels on the Nile by the Philae Temple and the £5 shows a pyramid scene.

periods of time. It is usually six years before a trainee engraver even gets around to touching a banknote plate.

The collector really does have something that took many years of training to produce. He has something that he can compare with other engravers, that he can form a judgement on, and assemble into a meaningful collection. Perhaps one great advantage over other aspects of collecting is that at the moment he does not pay a premium for collecting art on banknotes. Professional dealers relate their prices to rarity and demand. As most collectors concentrate on a series of notes or a particular

49 Detail of an American Bank Note Company engraving used on private bank issues, showing a buffalo hunt.

50 Two very rare collectors' items sold by Christie's in 1985, showing different styles of engraving: (**a**) Russo-Chinese Bank 100 Hong Ping Hua Pao Taels of 1907 and (**b**) Danish West Indies 100 francs of 1905.

country, there is no extra premium for a beautiful note, just because of its beauty – at the moment!

Remember too that as far as the printer is concerned, it costs no more to produce a £1,000 note than it does to produce a £1 note. The quality of workmanship is of the same high standard on low denominations as it is on the very high values. So the collector can indulge in his hobby without necessarily having to acquire high denominations.

While a lot of engravings on banknotes are faithful copies of famous paintings and so on, many are original, designed specifically for the notes. The major security firms employ their

51 Banca Italo-Germanica 1000 lire certificate of deposit 187 – showing Germanica and Italia with four cherubs. The actual size is 329 × 140mm. A particularly fine engraving.

own designers and art departments, but very occasionally use outside designers. Such a case occurred in 1979 when a private artist's work was used on the notes of Sri Lanka (formerly Ceylon) for some very unusual designs depicting the birds, animals and fishes of the nation.

An incredible amount of backroom work can go into preparing designs for banknotes. In 1819 the Bank of England approved one of Applegarth and Cowper's designs for a banknote, after they had received a number to examine. An Act of Parliament was passed just for this note, to make it illegal for anyone to copy the design, and by 1821 the Bank had spent £40,000 developing the printing – a quite staggering figure for that period of time. The finished product was handed to the Bank of England's 'backroom' department to see how easily they could forge the note. It was found that they could do so easily, and the whole design was dropped.

The current £10 note is such an everyday sight that few people really notice the design. Yet the portrait of Florence Nightingale, only one of several engravings on the note, took weeks to prepare even before it reached the engravers. The artist used three different photographs; taking the dress from one, the pose from another and the head from yet a third. The result, one might say, is an original masterpiece.

Of course not all notes are engraved, but generally the experts feel that it is the hardest form of artwork to counterfeit. Intaglio printing is easily recognised by the novice, as the raised ink on the engraved print can be felt, whereas a picture printed by lithography is flat. However, modern notes are often a combination of various forms of printing; again with a view to making the counterfeiting even harder. Three processes, lithography, letterpress and intaglio are nowadays frequently found on the same note.

To get the full appreciation of an engraved banknote the art-collector needs a magnification of times ten. Under such magnification one can see the fine detail of the graver's cuts. Each line is composed of many tiny cuts, each normally double cut, yet the whole is so delicately done that it looks like a straight one stroke line. The depth of cuts affect the shading and highly trained engravers are using micron measurements with an almost unbelievable accuracy.

Sometimes an engraver, very proud of the end-product, will work his own initials into the scroll-work or hide them in the design. Robert Austin, who succeeded Stephen Gooden in producing designs for the Bank of England, carefully inserted the letter 'A' into the £1 note. Unfortunately for collectors, and for him, it was noticed by meticulous bank officials and was ordered to be deleted before the issue was produced.

One device that has really troubled the counterfeiter is the 'latent' printing technique. Bradbury, Wilkinson and Co. have a special film used to show customers the security steps taken and this film was once shown to members of the International Bank Note Society. It revealed that letters, such as the initials of the printing company, are actually engraved into the side of a cut made by the graver as part of a normal line. Such tiny lettering, at such an angle, would not even be visible to normal examination. Even under high magnification it would not be noticed unless the area was correctly angled. Anyone trying to reproduce such a note photographically would totally miss the security device.

As with famous painters, it is often only after their death that an engraver's work is truly appreciated and collected. One of the greatest portrait engravers was John Harrison (no connection with the Harrison printing firm) who was responsible for many issues in the 1920s. Although he kept his independence as a freelance, he was so outstanding that he was Waterlow's chief portrait engraver. His portrait of Sun Yat Sen for Chinese notes has an animated quality that is hard for any artist to catch, and therefore won the approbation of successive Chinese officials. The Chinese liked it so much that even when they changed printers, they insisted on the same vignette being used – a situation which caused considerable embarrassment to the new printers. It was John Harrison who engraved the famous 500 escudo notes of Portugal which were the subject of a great forgery (see chapter 8).

Perhaps one great advantage for the collector of art on notes is his ability to display attractively. Common Spanish notes of the 1920–30 period show paintings by famous masters. Postcards or photographs of the original paintings mounted alongside the engraved note make an impressive display. Some collectors will photograph a portion of a note and enlarge it so that the graver's cuts can be seen clearly. Mounted with the note in an album, the effect is well worth the effort.

Fortunately for collectors many of the earlier notes have the name of the engraver on them, otherwise identifying some engravers of the eighteenth and early nineteenth centuries would be almost impossible. But the newcomer to the hobby will have enough work just learning to recognise the different printing firms! Even in modern times famous printers often leave their names off the notes 'to order'. Because of political upheavals, a country may not want the name of a 'capitalist' printing works to appear on its notes.

Certain printing techniques can be quickly recognised, for example, it will not be long before the collector notices the distinctive style of French printers. The notes too are very colourful and bright, good examples being the Laos 100 kip with its colourful dragons and portrait of the old King, and the French 100 francs depicting Napoleon.

There are sufficient different portraits of Queen Elizabeth II to allow collectors to specialise in her portrait engravings. The Annigoni portrait, particularly well produced on Mauritius notes, is often considered to be the best. But there are many fine portraits including one on the Malaya and British Borneo notes, delicately engraved by Waterlow and Sons.

Jacob Perkins was probably one of the greatest of the engravers. Strangely, he was not primarily interested in engraving; his great passion was machinery and invention. Today he is chiefly remembered because his machinery was adopted by the

52 Uruguay, Banco Ingles del Rio de la Plata, 100 pesos of 1862 showing
Minerva with shield and various animal vignettes. **53** Bank of Ethiopia 500
thaler note of 1932, depicting the Emperor in national dress and armed with
a rifle.

British Government for printing the first adhesive postage
stamps. But in 1795 George Washington signed the US patent
granted to Perkins for his Nail Making Machine which enabled
nails to be made at the rate of 20,000 a day instead of the possible
2,000 hand-forged tacks. (Nails were extremely important in the
pioneering days of America.)

Perkins came from Newburyport in Massachusetts and a

54 $100 of the Hong Kong & Shanghai Banking Corporation with unusual young head portrait of Queen Victoria and exceptionally rare 500 florin George V issue of East African Currency Board.

considerable collection can be made of his work under the various company names that he used. The problem of forgery led Perkins to experiment and develop ideas to combat counterfeiting. By 1803 he had developed a system which allowed a multiplicity of complex dies each interlocking precisely. Sometimes as many as

137

sixty-four die separations were used to form a picture. The key was to make them all line up perfectly, and this Perkins did. The effect on forgery was immediate. In 1809 the State of Massachusetts, which had suffered considerably from forgers, passed an Act which required all banknotes of the State to be printed by the new process developed by Perkins. He joined forces with a Colonel of Washington's Army, Gideon Fairman, a master craftsman whose engraving skill was just what Perkins needed to exploit his engineering developments. Steel plates last very much longer than the previous copper plates, but even these wore out and Perkins then developed the Master Die which enabled the die to be transferred as many times as was required.

When at the age of fifty Perkins became aware of the Bank of England's competition for an inimitable banknote, he set sail for England together with Fairman and they joined forces with Charles Heath, one of Britain's best known engravers at that time, to form 'Perkins, Fairman and Heath'. They did not succeed in getting the Bank of England contract, but they were soon printing a large proportion of the provincial banknotes, particularly in Scotland.

After some time Fairman decided to go back to the United States and his position was filled by Joshua Butters Bacon, a son-in-law of Perkins. Later H.P. Petch joined them to form 'Perkins, Bacon and Petch'. It is worth noting that all three were American citizens.

Another very famous engraver of British notes was Thomas Bewick, who began his apprenticeship in 1767 at the age of fourteen. He developed an extraordinary talent for wood-engraving and nothing has surpassed his illustrations in *History of British Birds*. It was this particular skill and a meticulous concern for detail that led to his involvement in banknote plates. He was approached by the Carlisle Bank to engrave copper plates and was later to recall: 'I lost no time beginning it. I had at that time never seen a ruling machine nor the beautiful engine-turning lately brought into use by Perkins, Fairman and Heath which were at that time I believe utterly unknown. I however proceeded with my plate and my object was to make a device look like a woodcut, and in this, though a first attempt, I succeeded. The number of impressions wanted were sent to Carlisle.'

Bradbury, Wilkinson Plc is the best known British firm of

security printers today. William Bradbury was born at Bakewell in 1799 and worked in Lincoln before moving to London in 1824 where he formed a printing company with William Dent. They were joined by Manning, but four years later the company became Bradbury and Evans, a partnership which was to last for more than forty years. Collectors will find many notes bearing their imprint. But it was William Bradbury's son, Henry, who gave the firm its great impetus through his particular talent as an engraver. At the age of nineteen he was sent to the Imperial Printing Office in Vienna to study and on his return began to introduce ideas which were to make the firm famous. The Wilkinson family had their roots in Lincolnshire. Many of the historical documents relating to the firm were lost through war damage but it is believed that Robert Wilkinson, a copper-plate engraver, worked with Henry Bradbury which led to the formation of Bradbury, Wilkinson and Co. in 1861. They were financed by Bradbury and Evans and were even permitted to use Bradbury and Evans plates for some of their first orders. They developed their business world-wide, but initially concentrated on South America and in 1871 received a major order of six million notes for Uruguay. It was an important year for Bradbury, Wilkinson and Co., for they then also started postage stamp engraving for Hyderabad and began its long association with the Crown Agents. In 1986 this famous firm was sold to De La Rue by its parent company, the American Bank Note Co.

I I

Notgeld

The new collector of paper money very soon comes across the word 'notgeld' and wonders what it means. It is a German word and very simply means 'emergency money' (**55**). To most collectors it means the fractional denominations issued by German towns, cities and even institutions and shops, during shortages of coin. The term came to be applied to similar issues by other nations. Later it was used to refer to German denominations issued privately (not by the State), for up to five billion marks.

The rise of notgeld in Germany started in 1914. Gradually the former note-issuing banks, the bankers for the twenty-five independent States, lost their right of issue to the Reichsbank and by 1914 only four other banks were allowed to issue notes: Badische Bank, Bayerische Notenbank, Sachsische Bank and Wurttembergische Notenbank, whose right of issue lasted until 1935.

With the threat of war in 1914, silver and gold were hoarded. Very quickly there was a desperate need for small change and over 450 towns and cities solved the problem by issuing small change notes. They had no legal right to do this as the prerogative of note-issue was that of the Reichsbank. However, the Reichsbank was well aware of the problems and turned a blind eye. These early notgeld issues are usually plain or with very simple ornamentation; there was no time to design the notes elaborately. Many were part-handwritten and a good number of the town councils sat up all night hand-signing notes. Mostly they were for denominations of fifty pfennigs, one, two and five marks, but other denominations exist, although they are much scarcer.

In August 1914 when war broke out, the Government issued Darlehenskassenschien (State Loan Bank Currency Notes) and informed city councils that there was now no further need of their notgeld issues and they were to be withdrawn. Only one city

55 German notgeld issues relating to former colonies.

failed to obey the Reichsbank notice and was fined. Some exceptions were permitted by the Reichsbank, such as Alsace, which was then occupied by French troops and some communities which had no revenue and needed to pay for State Relief. These notes were payable after the war and are generally very rare items today.

The State Loan notes and new coins performed their function well until 1916 when there was a new shortage of coin. The value of silver had risen dramatically and became greater than the nominal value of the coins. The State Loan notes for one, two and five marks served well for those denominations, but pfennigs

55 German notgeld issues to former colonies contd.

became unobtainable. The shortage first began in the East and gradually spread. This time the authorities had time to prepare and print well-designed notes, basically for five, ten, twenty-five and fifty pfennigs. Because they were for such small amounts, the notes attracted a number of collectors. It was not long before the local councils realised that they had a very good source of revenue.

Councils had to employ staff to reply to letters asking for notes. Although a few told the collectors they issued notes only for circulation, generally the extra revenue was too tempting. Soon some towns began issuing new sets and yet more sets to meet the

55 German notgeld issues to former colonies contd.

growing demand. Odd denominations like sixty, seventy-five, eighty and ninety pfennigs, which had little real use in day-to-day currency change needs, began to appear to tempt collectors. Despite the existence of State Loan notes, which were never in short supply, many councils issued one, two and five mark notes hoping that the Reichsbank would not do anything about it.

All these notes had a legitimate value and could be used for purchases, but by the 1920s there was no need for such a large amount of emergency money. Notes began to be very artistically designed and were issued in long sets. Often each note became one picture in a series, providing a picture-book story when the set was completed. Fairy tales, legends, town histories, the lives of the famous people of a town, were chosen as subjects. In the race to be bigger and better, some authorities issued as many as twelve different 50 pfennig notes at a time.

When it became apparent that many notes were issued solely for collectors, the Reichstag stepped in with legislation and a general prohibition order was made effective on 17 September 1922. Some notes continued to appear and led to prosecution, but in fact quite a number just happened to be printed at the time of the prohibition and had become valueless overnight – except to collectors.

Although the bulk of notgeld issues came from town authorities, there are a number of issues by factories, post offices and even police stations. In most cases they have a much higher value to modern collectors. A wide range of subjects is covered, including anti-Semitic issues, even obscene issues, and some famous German artists did pictures for notgeld. Some interesting signatures can also be found on notgeld – notably Dr Adenaur, Mayor of Cologne. There were some very unusual materials used apart from paper. Bielefeld issued many different types of note on silk (**56**) and uncut sheets of these were often used as table-cloths until their collector value got too high. Leather was frequently used and included the famous 'toe and heel' notes. The intention was that the 'note' would have an intrinsic value, and could be used to repair shoes, or spent. As inflation hit Germany the 'toe and heel' notes were soon worth over a million marks each for use in shoe-repair, which is why today they are extremely rare.

There are several different types of German notgeld: the 1914 issues fall into one category; later issues divide into the 1916 emergency notes, genuinely needed, and the series sets aimed at collectors, which were not really needed. Then there were postage-stamp notes, including some slotted into paper folders as well as circular discs; doppelscheine notgeld capable of being cut in halves and quarters; and Reutergeld, a name given to a similar series of notes issued by seventy Mecklenburg communities showing the works of Fritz Reuter. Playing cards were cut up and printed on for use as notgeld, and from 1918 to 1919 large denomination notgeld were issued, and again during the inflation period high value notgeld supplemented the notes of the Reichsbank. In 1918 there was a strike at the Reichsbank printers. Foreseeing problems the Reichsbank invited cities and

56 Silk note from Bielefeld for 25 pfennigs.

towns to issue notes for five, ten, twenty and fifty marks.

One man who spent a lifetime cataloguing and studying the German notgeld issues was Dr Arnold Keller, a legendary name in the paper money world. Before his death he classified the great maze of German notes into distinctive areas as follows:

Category	Period	No. of cities, towns, etc., issuing notes
All notes	1914	452
Small notes	1916–1922	3,900
Serial notes	1921–1922	874
Large notes	1918–1919	624

He further categorised inflation notes of German towns and cities into the following: inflation 1922, 715 cities; inflation 1923, 5,900 cities. He also listed 587 prisoner of war camps, issuing 5,100 different notes. Yet another division of notgeld was made by Dr Keller for notes of constant value in 1923–4. He found 565 cities, issuing 3,950 different notes. Many of these are quite scarce, as in order to have a constant value they tended to be tied to the Goldmark or the US Dollar.

Today all notgeld is collected regardless of whether it was primarily issued for collectors or for circulation. The notes tell a story of German history and of a craze for collecting which swept Germany at that time. At the time, Dr Keller edited and published a magazine, *Das Notgeld*, which listed spurious issues – themselves of great interest to collectors today. Speculators would buy the right of issue from various communities and a virtual stock exchange grew up for dealing in them. This notgeld exchange, in Hamburg, was once raided by the police and temporarily closed. In Schleswig-Holstein one enterprising character by the name of Appel printed notgeld for various issuers but duplicated the orders for himself. One man persuaded about forty towns in Pinneberg district to issue sets and sell them all to him. Some speculators did not see the need to pay out money like that, and simply invented notgeld themselves. Chief among these was Appel himself, who even signed some notes 'Leppa' (Appel backwards). It was Dr Keller who unravelled all this information while studying numismatics at the University of München under Professor Buchenau (he also studied oriental languages). He met some of the pioneer collectors of these notes, Lejeune, Dr Schoeller and the great Adolf Rosenblatt, who designed the first album for notgeld collectors. But his most important contact was the great collector, General Consul Rotmann in Bremen. Dr Keller actually turned down a request from Rotmann to exchange notes because Rotmann was an extremely wealthy man. But Rotmann wrote again and later in 1920 Dr Keller was invited to stay at Rotmann's home where two secretaries were employed for no other purpose than to write letters for obtaining notgeld specimens for his collection. Much later Rotmann was to lose his fortune and his entire collection was purchased by Dr Keller.

While one often hears collectors say that there are millions of notgeld, the truth is that there are probably just over 120,000 different issues. The vast majority can be bought today for between 15 and 25 pence which makes it an ideal area for collectors who do not wish to spend too much on individual notes. There are many volumes to Dr. Arnold Keller's *Das Deutsche Notgeld* and the complete work would cost over £100, but the majority of the notes encountered by collectors today will be found in Volume IV *Serienscheine*, a three hundred page book with nearly fifty pages of illustrations. It normally retails at £15 and is published by Battenberg. There is also an invaluable booklet published by Manor Press called *Notgeld Handbook No. 1*, which is an English translation of the main prefaces to Dr Arnold Keller's works. It normally retails at £2.50.

12

Modern Notes

Modern history is reflected on banknote issues and collectors have the advantage of being able to get them as they are issued, and before any rarity value is attached. A collection of modern notes of the world can be made into a picture gallery of events. In South America current issues show the wild spread of inflation and the changing units of currency in an effort to wipe out some of the zeros that would otherwise have to appear on the notes. In Africa the continual struggles for leadership are reflected in the changes of the portraits.

Notes picturing a deposed leader tend to be taken out of circulation quickly by the incoming authority and are sometimes destroyed, so can become scarce very quickly. A very good example of this is Iran. The multitude of issues that followed the overthrow of the Shah has meant that there are some very rare modern notes. The first note a collector needs to get hold of is one signed by Ali-Reza Nobari, Governor of the Bank Markazi, and Abol Hassan Banisadr, President of Iran. Banisadr was simply told: 'You are no longer President of Iran' and fled. The story of Nobari is interesting to collectors of paper money as he was interviewed by Western journalists after his escape.

The first inkling that anything was wrong came when Mrs Nobari checked in her luggage at the airport to fly back to Iran and then telephoned his office to let him know she was coming. It was 8 June 1981. There was no reply. In Iran in 1981, that was ominous. She hastily got her luggage off the plane and stayed put. Nobari's office was crowded with revolutionaries, armed to the teeth. Nobari was on the death list. But he had been too quick for them and was in hiding with friends and about to embark on a five-month trek to the Kurdish border with Turkey and to freedom. He is still in hiding.

Banknotes were a major cause of his rift with Ayatollah Ruhollah Khomeini. The long struggle between Khomeini and the Shah, ending with the taking of American hostages is well known, but the impact the Ayatollah had on banknote production was nearly as great and threatened to cause a breakdown in day to day banking facilities.

On taking power the Ayatollah lost no time in declaring that paper money with the portrait of the Shah was to be invalidated, and the population were given three months to turn in the notes. The Bank of Tehran hurriedly overstamped the portrait of the Shah with crosses, some in blue and others in red. Every Shah note, including much earlier note issues with young head portraits, was treated this way. Some of the more fanatical followers put their own private obliterations over the Shah. A selection of these is worth including in a collection though only those of the Bank of Tehran can ever be expected to go up in value.

In a near bankrupt Iran the printing of new money would take time and planning, so the Ayatollah was persuaded that the existing money should still be used, but with an overprint obliterating the Shah's head. An elaborate arabesque design was produced which very efficiently obliterated the Shah's portrait. In order to keep the flow of paper money going a number of different printers were used and collectors will find shades of black and green. Clearly a printing machine was in the bank, for records show high-denomination notes being turned in and returned to the holder with the overprint added. Many errors occurred. Often the note would be put through the machine the wrong way up causing the obliteration to fall on the non-portrait side of the note. In such cases the note was simply put through again and issued with a double overprint.

While all this was going on one of the Ayatollah's officials noticed that the watermark on the notes still proudly displayed the Shah's head. Some of the notes had already been put back in circulation; those that had not, and new supplies, were hurriedly given a second overprint which consisted of a lion and sun emblem over the watermark area as well as the Shah portrait obliteration. This new overprint was the ancient symbol of Persia and it did not please the Ayatollah, as it reminded him of the Shahs. The overprint was immediately dropped from the notes, which continued to circulate with just the head obliteration until a new overprint, a calligraphic inscription for 'Islamic Republic of Iran' was brought into use.

Nobari was getting more and more disillusioned, as all these interruptions were destroying his attempt to keep the money supply flowing for daily use. Then came another blow from the Ayatollah. All the Shah notes were to be withdrawn and replaced with a totally new issue of notes. Designing new banknotes and engraving the steel plates takes a long time. The Governor of the Bank tried to overcome the time delays by using much of the design in the former issues and in some denominations literally only changing the design part which showed the Shah's portrait, which now became a view of the Emam Reza Mosque. These notes were therefore produced very quickly compared to normal production. It was perhaps fortunate for Iran that some of their engravers were undergoing instruction at Bradbury, Wilkinson's at the time, and were now competent for the task.

However, Nobari recalled that he had many other banking problems on his mind at this time. The Ayatollah's total rejection of the principle of charging interest led him to require all loans to be paid up. It was Christmas for some American bankers who had lent money at much lower rates than the current prevailing rate. They were paid up and able to re-lend elsewhere at the higher rate.

While trying to keep Iran's financial problems under control while all this was going on, Nobari overlooked the distaste the Ayatollah had shown for the earlier lion and sun emblem which had been used as an overprint. To most people it was simply a national emblem and the new notes had the device on them. It did not escape the eagle eye of the Ayatollah. The notes had just come in time to fill the ever increasing gap in money supply. Nobari was congratulating himself on overcoming the paper money shortage. Suddenly he was up against a brick wall. The new notes, he was told, would not do. They were not to be circulated until the offensive emblem had been obliterated. In vain the bank officials argued that the emblem was a national symbol of ancient Persia and had nothing to do with the deposed Shah.

The notes were now sent to over twenty different printing firms who were set to work day and night overprinting the watermark area on both sides of the note. The work was done in Tehran and one inscription seal reads: 'Islamic Republic of Iran' (obverse) and the other a revolutionary emblem. Naturally this rush has caused many varieties and errors. Information is still coming in, but it is known that the 200 and 500 rials have been overprinted in green, olive, black, red-brown and brown. The 1,000 rials is known with black and brown overprints and the 5,000 with violet. The highest denomination, the 10,000, is known in green or brown.

Although it is not easy to see the watermark or design under the new overprint with normal eyesight, it has been reported from Iran that some paper was accidentally used which still had the Shah's head in the watermark. So there are two types to look for among specialists; those with the lion emblem underneath and those with the Shah watermark. More new notes were added, the high denominations, five and ten thousand rials showing a procession of revolutionaries carrying placards with a picture of the Ayatollah on them. These were the last notes to be signed by Nobari. The writing was on the wall and he went into hiding. These notes have now all been replaced by new signatures or totally new notes, showing Mullahs at prayer and so on. At the end of 1985 a new hundred rial note was issued showing S. Hassan Modarres, who was in fact responsible for helping to put the Shah on the throne, though he was subsequently imprisoned by the Shah. It has since been withdrawn.

This whole series of notes gives the collector a fine opportunity to make a special study and look for errors and varieties. At present they will be at nominal prices, but once fully catalogued some of them are likely to become much more expensive. For instance, the 200 rials was first issued with a design of six-pointed stars on the reverse. Because of the Jewish connection these were changed to twelve-pointed stars. Various signature combinations were used, and changes in the metal strip which cause a number of varieties. Add to this that some of the signatories were shot on the orders of the Ayatollah and replaced, and the whole area becomes a complicated but interesting field of study.

Signature combinations on notes can be very important as far as rarity is concerned. A good example of this is the issues of Sierre Leone (Mountain of the Lion). Each note is signed by five different people and paper money researcher David August compiled a list of the signatories found on notes between 1964 and 1979. They are:

Governors	*Deputy Governors*
Gordon E. Hall.	S.B. Nicol-Cole
S.B Nicol-Cole	S.L. Bangura
S.L. Bangura	A.S.C. Johnson
A.S.C. Johnson	M.R. Tejan-Cole

Directors

Dr M.C.F. Eason	H. Eccles-James
Dr Davidson S.W.H. Nicol	Ven. Archdeacon M. Keili
Dr Claude Nelson-Williams	Dr Sheka S. Magona
Bai Sherbro S.B. Komkanda II	G.L.V. Williams
S. Matturi	Paramount Chief Massayeli
T.S. Johnson	Tham.
Dr S.M. Broderick	
Dr W.H. Fitzjohn	

Each note is signed by the Governor, Deputy Governor and three directors. The exact dating can be done by signature changes which occurred as the Board of Directors changed composition. The first notes of Sierra Leone, one, two and five leones (Pick 1, 2 and 3) are also a good example of under-cataloguing. The first two catalogued at $8 and $15 respectively for years. The 1986 Pick now reflects auction prices at $50 and $75. The true rarity of signature combinations is yet to be established.

The changing face of Africa is reflected in the portraits on notes (**57, 58**). In 1973 Uganda issued a series of notes with a portrait of Idi Amin. These were replaced after he was forced to flee the country. For a time there were considerable quantities of these notes on the market but they are gradually drying up and today it is hard to get the higher denominations at all. His portrait shows him bemedalled (he awarded himself the VC for destroying the British Empire).

Another infamous character on banknotes is ex-President Bokassa of the Central African Republic. He indulged in several portraits of himself on banknotes (**59**). On the occasion that he spent three-quarters of the national income on his Napoleonic style wedding, he even changed the name of the country to 'Empire Centrafricain' which also appears on a series of notes, now very scarce. Shortly after that the French authorities deposed him following the machine-gunning of some school

57 Idi Amin on a 5 shilling note of Uganda before he was deposed.

58 Ghana obtained independence on 6 March 1957 (formerly the Gold Coast and British Togoland) and was the first Negro African Colony to do so. Its first leader, Kwame Nkrumah, claimed to be a God and was overthrown by the army and police in 1966.

children who were not wearing the correct uniform. His portrait also appears on Equatorial African States notes.

Collectors will soon find that many of the African leaders were not so lucky as Amin and Bokassa, and some met violent deaths. In Equatorial Guinea the notes from 1975 to 1979 show the portrait of President M.N. Biyogo. He was murdered and new notes hurriedly introduced without his portrait. New notes were in

59 Emperor Bokassa pictured on a 500 franc note of the Central African Republic. He was deposed by the French after he had murdered some school-children.

Bipkwele denominations as against the earlier ekuele system, and note issues of much earlier dates were overprinted in the new currency but were not issued as the new notes were delivered in time. They have been released in quantity for collectors.

During his term of office Biyogo changed his name, and this has caused some scarce banknotes. Collectors will easily identify the change; under the portrait his name is given with three words; with the change of name, five words appear (**60**). The high denomination, 1,000 ekuele, is only known in prefix A/1 and A/2 and the A/2 series is scarce as it only reached approximately 300,000 of the million run before his murder and the invalidation of his notes.

Katanga notes, of which only ten different types were ever issued, reflect the bloody fighting that ended in the reintegration of Katanga into the Republic of the Congo. The leader, Moise Tshombe, was murdered (**61**). All his notes are rare; not one catalogues at less than $100 in uncirculated condition and yet they were issued from 1960 until 1962. Collectors who were collecting current notes at the time were picking them up for a pound or two.

Biafra was another African territory with a short life. Lieutenant-Colonel E.O. Ojukwu, Military Governor of the Eastern Region of Nigeria, proclaimed the Republic of Biafra on 30 May

60 1,000 ekuele with a portrait of murdered Biyogo. Earlier issues had a three-word name under the portrait instead of five.

61 Moise Tshombe, murdered leader of the break-away Katanga nation, from the Republic of the Congo.

1967. Notes were issued in the same year showing a palm tree and rising sun. Some of these are still common; 5s., 10s., £1, £5 and £10 were issued with two separate issues of the 5s. and £1. After very heavy fighting the new country surrendered on 15 January 1970. These notes were produced in a hurry and we are still learning about them. The archivist Mr R. Seaman has made a special study of the area philatelically and in the course of his investigations learned that a £20 note had also been prepared. Whether it was issued at all is not known.

62 President Numeiri wearing national head-dress on a 50 piastre note of Sudan. He was deposed in 1985.

The changeover of Rhodesia to Zimbabwe has left a lot of interesting material for collectors of paper money. From 1979 the notes of the Reserve Bank of Rhodesia deleted the watermark of Cecil Rhodes and replaced it with the Zimbabwe bird. New notes of Zimbabwe depicted the Matapos Rocks. There are some rarities. An error led to Cecil Rhodes watermarked paper being used for a few notes. Also the name of the city of Salisbury was changed to Harare and collectors can find the different names on Zimbabwe notes dated the same year.

More recently the notes of Sudan issued in 1981 and showing President Numeiri wearing national headdress (**62**) have suddenly been withdrawn. He was overthrown while out of the country, in 1985.

New notes were recently issued by the BEAC (Bank of Central African States), and these have been withdrawn almost before they started to circulate! The 1,000 franc note had been printed in France and shows a map of Chad with its northern, rebel-held territory, omitted (**63**). The map shows the bank's member nations: Chad, Cameroon, Central African Republic, Gabon, Equatorial Guinea and Congo. The Chadian government was furious to find the Libya-backed part of Chad, held by rebels since 1983, was missing, and demanded the withdrawal of the note. This was authorised by the BEAC.

Whether or not these notes will find their way out to collectors

63 One of the Bank of Central African States notes which has a common design to the nations in the Central African Franc zone. Chad objected because the map did not show the rebel-held part of Chad and the whole issue has been withdrawn.

64 Haiti issued new notes in 1986 with the portrait of Jean Claude Duvalier, the son of 'Papa Doc', whose portrait appears on previous issues. Duvalier was forced to flee the country soon after the issue of notes, which are likely to become scarce collectors' items. In view of the hatred in which he was held, it is expected the notes will be withdrawn from circulation – the people dug up his father and 'danced on his bones'!

65 After the turmoil in the Philippines in 1986 which led to President Marcos being forced to leave the country, collectors may like to get the 10 piso 1981 issue which has an overstamp portrait of President Marcos commemorating his inauguration as President in that year. All Philippine notes from 1966 have the Marcos signature on them.

or whether the intended destruction will make them rarities is not known yet, but collectors of modern notes would do well to try and get one of each. The notes were quickly replaced with the identical design except that the map of Chad now continues into the top margin. Whilst Africa had been used to show the type of things that happen to note issues, the same principle really applies to other areas and research collectors can have a lot of enjoyment tracing the affairs of South and Central America, and elsewhere.

Societies

The **International Banknote Society** is the most useful for collectors in the UK. Membership applications can be made to:
London branch: Suresh Gupta, 11 Middle Row, London W1O 5AT;
Burnley branch: Francis Thornton, 49 Brier Crescent, Nelson, Lancs BB9 0QD;
Nottingham branch: Roy Spick, 112 Long Lane, Attenborgh, Nottingham NG6 6BW.

The society has about 2,000 members, produces a quarterly magazine, runs postal auctions and has regular meetings world-wide. An annual European congress is held in London. The IBNS also has details of a number of specialist societies.

The **Society of Paper Money Collectors** in the USA produces a bimonthly magazine and principally deals with North American paper money.

The World Paper Currency Collector, a world-wide society but based in the USA, publishes *The Currency Collector*, a quarterly magazine.

The **American Numismatic Association** (ANA) is the biggest numismatic association, with a monthly magazine covering mostly coins, but including some banknotes. The ANA shows are also mainly for coin collectors, but now about forty per cent of dealers carry banknotes too.

The **Latin American Paper Money Society** publishes *Lansa* – a bilingual English and Spanish magazine, three times a year.

The **Psywar Society** covers psychological war documents, propaganda of all sorts, including notes.

Museums can be a useful source of information for collectors and archivists can also be very helpful. Collectors owe a lot to archivists, as they have the source material to examine, and their published findings can be invaluable to the collecting world. Most of the major banks have archivists, and many of them go out of their way to be helpful to collectors.

APPENDIX B

The Library

As with all hobbies, banknote enthusiasts have a 'Bible', *The Standard Catalog of World Paper Money*, by Albert Pick, published by Krause Publications Inc. The current (fifth) edition, is in two volumes. Volume 1 deals with 'specialised issues' (private banks, etc), while Volume 2 is for 'general issues' (official government issues, etc). They cost £37.50 each, but between them have pictures of 17,000 notes and list over 37,000 notes. They are indispensable to the serious collector. The vast majority of notes which come into the hands of a new collector will be easily traceable in Pick. Values in US dollars are given for three grades. Unlike the philatelic world, where one often hears people talking about 'half cat.' or even less, the Pick catalogues are very accurate in reflecting market trends. This is because for every edition sections of the catalogue are sent out to specialists for their opinions, which are then put together by the catalogue editors, Colin Bruce and Neil Shafer. Such errors as there are, occur when an inflation completely alters the values of the notes, or if a hoard of old notes suddenly comes on the market, making notes common which were previously rare.

Specialists in Bank of England and Treasury notes have a recognised 'Bible' of their own. *English Paper Money* by Vincent Duggleby, published by Stanley Gibbons Publications Ltd, and edited by Colin Narbeth, is now in its third edition and costs £7.50. It includes details down to the rarity of individual prefix letters and values are given for VF and EF. A consortium of dealers are approached to fix the prices, headed by Britain's best known specialist in this field, David Keable. The prices are therefore a very good guide for the new collector. The book also contains chapters on production, design, etc.

Scottish notes are very popular and the standard work of reference is *Scottish Banknotes* by the late James Douglas, published by Stanley Gibbons Publications Ltd, and priced at £5. It is now only obtainable second-hand and is likely to cost £9. It covers all the known issues of Scotland with historical pieces about each bank. Douglas also completed the first volume of a series of books of a more specialised nature. This is *20th Century Scottish Banknotes Volume 1*, dealing with the Bank of Scotland, British Linen Bank and Union Bank, and is as definitive as anything can get, even giving the exact number of each note printed. There is a valuation code in the form of a bookmark, so that it can be up-dated without the owner having to buy a new book. Published by Banking Memorabilia of Carlisle, it costs £9.50 as a softback. The second volume, dealing with the Royal Bank and its subsidiaries, was completed by one of the great collectors of Scottish notes, Dr R.W. Pringle, and was published in 1986.

Another very popular field of collecting is military notes, and there is a very good catalogue, *World War II Military Currency* by C. Frederick Schwan and Joseph E. Boling, published by BNR Press, South Carolina in 1978. It is packed with information, but is out-of-print, and second-hand copies fetch anything up to £15. The prices are no longer accurate, but the rarity ratio between prices is a very sound guide.

Chinese Banknotes by Ward D. Smith and Brian Matravers is the only comprehensive guide (apart from Pick) for Chinese notes, but again is out of print. Published by Shirjieh Publishers, California, in 1970, its range is far greater than Pick as it covers many private issues. The major fault is that it can be difficult to look something up; however the International Bank Note Society produced a special Alphabetical Cross-Index to be used with the book.

There are many books dealing with highly specialised subjects, such as *Philippine Emergency and Guerilla Currency of World War II*, by Neil Shafer, 464 pages, Western Publishing Co. Inc., USA, price $15, with great detail about each issue.

Books useful to single-country collectors exist for most of the major nations. Germany, in particular, is well covered as there has always been a strong following of collectors of German paper money, for example the late Dr Arnold Keller, who undertook the formidable task of cataloguing all German notgeld, which fills six volumes, one or two of them nearly two inches thick. The major current work on German notes is *Papiergeld-spezialkatalog Deutschland 1874–1980*, published by Battenberg and authored by Pick/Rixen. Whereas Pick's standard catalogue lists all the note types, works such as these go into serial prefixes and varieties in great depth. There is also *Die Banknoten Des Deutschen Reiches AB 1871* by Holger Rosenberg – one of the best known dealers in Germany – which costs around £5 for the 1985 edition. Another well-known authority is Dieter Hoffmann, author of *Das Notenbuch*, a catalogue of German banknotes from 1874, which costs about £10.

Italy is well represented by authors such as Adolfo Mini, whose *La Carta Moneta Italiana 1746–1960*, published in 1967, is out of print and fetching about £22. The best book on Italian notes, now in two volumes, is undoubtedly the giant-sized full colour work by the Banca Popolare di Novara, which does not appear to have ever been sold through bookshops, and sells for about £150 when a second-hand copy becomes available.

Some of the smaller countries also have very fine books covering the paper money issues. Finland has a 656-page book, *Suomessa kaytetyt rahat*, by Erkki Borg, printed by Kirjapaino Oy Nov in 1976, and Denmark has *Danmarks officielle Penge sedler 1713–1983*, published by Dansk Numismatisk Forening. Most of these books have English translations.

The International Bank Note Society has also published a number of volumes dealing with specific subjects, such as Paper Money of Japan, Straits Settlements, British North Borneo, Sarawak, Rubber Export Coupons, the Japanese occupation of Malaya, and Belgium and its colonies.

There are a number of books which do not *list* notes, but just give information about their issues, particularly those by the late Edward Kann, who was a banker in China for many years. His *Ancient Paper Money of China* and *Government Banks of China*, were published in English by Transatlantic Authors Ltd, and fetch £5 to £6 a volume.

Other books which are very useful to specialists include Gaytan's *Paper Currency of Mexico*, *Les Assignats* by Jean La Faurie, and *The Early Paper Money of America* by Eric P. Newman – a very thorough catalogue of the earliest notes of America and the War of Independence.

Only a few books have been mentioned but the new collector can get a full listing of books and articles covering a specific subject from the International Bank Note Society librarian. Other books of interest are *The Bank of England Note* by A.D. Mackenzie, Cambridge University Press, 1953; and *Banks, Bankers and Banking in Northumberland, Durham and North Yorkshire*, by Maberly Phillips, published in 1894, and fetching as much as £150. Most of the major banks in the British Isles have published their own histories, and many of them picture rare and little known banknote issues.

Collectors of British notes issued by provincial banks have only one catalogue available, *The Standard Catalogue of Provincial Banks and Banknotes* by G.L. Grant, published by Spink. It retails at £9.75 and while it does not pretend to be complete, is a major pioneering work essential to collectors of this series. Then there is *Banknotes and Banking in the Isle of Man, 1788–1970* by Ernest Quarmby, also published by Spink. *Banks and Banknotes of Exeter, 1769–1906* is another specialist work, by John Royton, published privately in 1984.

Three major British publications have worth-while sections which deal with paper money:

Coin and Medal News, is a monthly publication, edited by John W. Mussell and published by Token Publishing Ltd, Crossways Road, Grayshott, Hindhead, Surrey GU26 6HF. It costs 90p.

Coin Monthly, another monthly, is edited by Charmaine Swartz and is published by Numismatic Publishing Co., Sovereign House, Brentwood, Essex, CM14 4SE. It costs 99p.

Bond and Banknote News, is a bi-monthly, edited by Michael Veissid and published by Squirrel Publishing Ltd, Hobsley House, Frodesley, Dorrington, Shrewsbury SY5 7HD. It costs £1.

Back copies of these magazines are well worth getting in order to build up a library of technical articles which the collector can then index to suit his own needs. Such magazines are also valuable because of all the advertisements from dealers of the world.

A good library is a store-house of knowledge that the collector can refer to at any time and being able to identify a scarce variety can lead to a number of bargains, which can pay for the library over and over again.

Index